DICTIONARY OF GIFTED, TALENTED, & CREATIVE EDUCATION TERMS

Mary M. Frasier

Jo Ann Carland

Trillium Press

New York

To Jim, Trey & Jason Carland
Richard, Mariel, & Deirdre Frasier

Trillium Press
Box 921
Madison Square Station
New York NY 10159
(212) 684-7399

ISBN: 0-89824-021-2
Printed in the United States of America

TABLE OF CONTENTS

PREFACE

In any new or emerging specialized field, new terms must be invented and old terms assume specialized meanings. The field of Gifted, Talented, and Creative Education is one of those emerging fields and communication within the field as well as between the field and other groups is frequently difficult and confusing. Thus, the need for a dictionary and reference book of terms used in the field is important. In this book, Mary M. Frasier and Jo Ann Carland have done a useful and pioneering job in trying to meet this need.

The main body of this book consists of the definitions of the key terms in the field of Gifted, Talented, and Creative Education. Primary sources have been used and cited and in most cases more than one definition has been offered. In some cases, the alternative definitions enrich one another or say the same things in slightly different terms. In some cases, they deal with different facets of the term or concept.

Besides the main body of terms, this dictionary contains reference appendices on tests frequently used to identify children for gifted programs and on major organizations. Included is a bibliography of the original sources for the terms used. Such a dictionary and collection of resources should be especially useful for graduate students and school systems, as well as for parents and the public in general.

The field of Gifted, Talented, and Creative Education has many roots and draws upon many disciplines. Similarly, writers in the field have been trained in very diverse fields. Some have been trained in Educational Psychology or Special Education. Others have been trained in the arts, business, psychiatry, the sciences, and many other fields. Their training in these disciplines gives their writings a variety of special flavors despite the fact that their professional identification may now be in Gifted, Talented, and Creative Education. This great diversity enriches the field and at the same time makes important an understanding of key terms and concepts.

In addition to assisting students, teachers, parents, school administrators, and parents with their study, employment, research, and writing in the field of Gifted, Talented, and Creative Education, it is hoped that this work will help to standardize usage of the terms in this vigorous and rapidly maturing field.

E. Paul Torrance
Department of Educational Psychology
University of Georgia
February 1981.

AUTHOR'S INTRODUCTION

This dictionary offers examples of the usage of the major terms employed in the education of gifted, talented, and creative children. To accomplish this, pertinent journal articles and books written since 1960 were searched to develop a comprehensive list of terms important to those in the field.

In each case, the terms are defined in the words of experts in the field. For the most part, these quotations are exactly as originally published. In a very few instances, we had to make minor alterations in the interests of brevity and clarity.

The aim here was to include only those definitions we thought would be helpful to students, educators, and administrators in the field of education. We included the main current usage or usages, and any subsidiary uses that were clearly important. We made no judgment as to which definitions or descriptions were correct, nor did we explore the history of the uses of these terms.

Mary Frasier
Jo Ann Carland

A

AAG (See American Association for the Gifted, The; Appendix B)

ABBREVIATED BINET FOR DISADVANTAGED
An abbreviated version of the Binet favoring the southeastern Black disadvantaged student.
Bruch, 1971, 268.

ABDA: (See Abbreviated Binet for Disadvantaged)

ABILITY
The actual power present in an organism to carry to completion any given act or to make adjustments successfully, the response being subject to voluntary control and dependent on the motivation of the subject to do his best performance.
Good, 1973, 1.

ABILITY, COGNITIVE (See Intelligence)

ABILITY GROUPING
1. ...is a provision that allows some students to be separated from the more typical students by some given criteria, in this case, the level of measured intelligence. Ability grouping may be implemented as special classes or schools, special groups, meeting prior to or after school, pullout programs during school hours where gifted students are separated for a given period of time and then returned to the regular program or summer workshops. At the secondary level, a tracking system is often used to group students into classes based on academic ability.
Clark, 1979, 139.
2. The practice of organizing classroom groups in a graded school to put together children of a given age and grade who have most nearly the same standing on measures or judgments of learning achievement or capability....Ability grouping may be based on a single test, on teacher judgment, or on a composite of several tests and/or judgments.
Findley & Bryan, 1970, 2.
3. Grouping of pupils within classes or schools on the basis of some measured mental ability.
Good, 1973, 269.
4. (A procedure whereby) a given grade is divided into different classes on the basis of ability, the range of ability within each class being relatively narrow.
Hopke, 1968, 3.

5. An administrative delivery system used widely in educating the gifted. Students are divided into homogeneous groups based upon student performance in meeting set criteria necessary for participation in a particular group.

Walker, 1978, 489.

6. Refers to removal of children from heterogeneous classroom settings to classrooms composed of children with similar ability levels.

Suran & Rizzo, 1979, 487.

7. Grouping of children to any single criterion such as reading ability or mental age (intelligence).

Torrance, 1965, 38.

8. Also sometimes called "segregation." The practice of assembling or deploying students for instructional purposes who are somewhat nearer together in general capacity for learning, or in given specific aptitudes, so that instruction and learning may proceed at a pace and in terms of qualities suited to this (these) capacities. Contrasts with those forms of grouping which use chronological age or alphabet as criteria for homogeneity and developmental readiness. May take the form of special classes, special schools, multiple track curricula, etc, and may be arranged for part or for all of the school curriculum. Specific capacities for differing areas of knowledge or skill, with interests related thereto, are recognized as superior criteria for grouping, as opposed to general indices (e.g. composite I.Q.) applied across the range of school activities.

SREB Report, 1962, 29.

ABILITY TEST

A nontechnical term usually applied to tests designed to measure intelligence or aptitude; ordinarily used with various modifying adjectives, for example, mechanical ability test or musical ability test.

Good, 1973, 594.

ABLE

1. A term used to describe a child whose rate of development with respect to time on some variable of social significance is significantly larger than that of the general population of children.

Gowan & Demos, 1964, 33.

2. Used to describe a pupil of high learning ability.

Hopke, 1968, 4.

ABOVE-AVERAGE GIFTED
115+ IQ.
> Worcester, 1956, 4.

ABSTRACT REASONING TEST
Any test of abstract-reasoning ability; any test designed to measure capacity for solving problems requiring facility in the use of abstract symbols.
> Good, 1973, 594.

ACADEMIC ACHIEVEMENT
Knowledge attained or skills developed in school subjects, usually designated by test scores or by marks assigned by teachers, or by both.
> Good, 1973, 7.

ACADEMICALLY GIFTED, THE
Individuals possessing superior general intellectual ability or specific aptitude are referred to as the academically gifted. IQ scores often are the major determinant in identifying academically gifted students.
> Walker, 1978, 472.

ACADEMIC APTITUDE
1. The ability of a person to deal in abstractions and to engage successfully in activities that involve literary or classical learning experiences.
> Good, 1973, 37.

2. The combination of native and acquired abilities that is needed for school work; likelihood of success in mastering academic work, as estimated from measures of necessary abilities.   (Also called scholastic aptitude.)
> Hopke, 1968, 4.

ACADEMIC-APTITUDE TEST
A prognostic test designed to measure the fitness of the examinee to undertake and perform activities of an academic nature.
> Good, 1973, 594.

ACADEMICALLY TALENTED
Commonly used to describe the group qualified to complete undergraduate college work. This group comprises about the top 16% of the general population at a given age level and would start at a Stanford Binet IQ of 116. However, in some high socio-economic areas 116 could be average. (Also see Child,

Academically Talented.)
> Syphers, 1972, 5.

ACADEMIC PROMISE TEST: (See Appendix D)

ACCELERATED COLLEGE ENROLLMENT PROGRAM (ACE)
A program that allows gifted students to enroll in regular university programs on university campuses throughout the year and receive university credit which can be banked for use after high school graduation. Open to high school juniors and seniors.
> Clark, 1979, 215.

ACCELERATED MODEL, THE
A model where the child has access to advanced content. The child may be physically placed with older groups or remain with his peers. Traditional or typical content is ordinarily used in this model. Little new content is produced. The main advantage of this model is the preparation of the gifted for productivity earlier in life.
> Rice, 1970, 290.

ACCELERATION
1. Acceleration can take many forms. It can mean early entrance to formal schooling, moving through a primary area in two rather than three years, grade skipping, advanced placement, or moving through material at an accelerated rate. However it is implemented, it will result in student completion of formal schooling in less time than is usually required.
> Clark, 1979, 143.

2. Activities that promote learning beyond regularly prescribed curriculum. Examples of types of acceleration are: early grade promotion, advanced placement classes, ungraded classes, multi-age classes, tutoring, correspondence courses, extra classes for extra credit, credit by examination, independent study, continuous study curriculum, year round school, flexible scheduling, block or back-to-back classes.
> Correll, 1978, 25.

3. (a) The process of progressing through the school grades at a rate faster than that of the average child, either in skipping grades or by rapidly mastering the work of one grade and moving on to the next higher grade; (b) advancement in mental growth or achievement beyond the average for the individual's chronological age; (c) a general term including all administrative practices which result in completing a school

program in less than the usual time allotted.

Good, 1973, 4.

4. An endeavor to expedite the learning process and reduce the period of formal education.

Fliegler, 1961, 27.

5. A system whereby gifted children could proceed at their own rate of development through the grades. One of the purposes of accelerating a bright youngster has been to get him into a more competitive situation with children at his own level....Another major advantage of accelerating children, however, is to shorten the total time that they spend in the educational program.

Gallagher, 1966, 93-94.

6. Means to move ahead and have advanced placement. This process has been used for many years in different ways, but with a promising result. Acceleration may be accomplished at all levels of education including the following: early admission to elementary school, grade skipping, combining grades, shortening the duration of high school or junior high school, assumption of heavier programs, summer studies for high school and college; early admission for college, credit by examination during college. Authorities are in agreement that acceleration should not exceed two years in the twelve-year common school programs. Physical age and social maturity should be considered as well as academic achievement in accelerating a student.

Gold, 1965, 28.

7. This term is commonly applied to any means of advancing students through school faster than the standard pace of one year for each year of age. Some means of acceleration include: entering first grade early; being placed in rapid-advancement classes; taking extra courses, even college courses, in high school; being allowed to move ahead on an individual basis in ungraded classes; having short-term promotions in lower grades; lengthening the school year.

Hildreth, 1966, 276.

8. Refers to (a) admitting gifted children to kindergarten or first grade according to mental age rather than chronological age, (b) skipping grades, (c) telescoping grades, (d) early admission to secondary schools or colleges, and (e) other methods such as passing courses in high school and college by examination.

Kirk & Gallagher, 1979, 92.

9. Involves letting a student work at a higher grade level—for example, giving sixth-grade books to a fourth grader or even advancing him into a sixth grade class.

Maeroff, 1978, 171.

10. Providing a program whereby a particular child may progress

more rapidly than does the average. Acceleration, educationally speaking, is the provision for an individual to progress comfortably at the speed for which he is built.

Worcester, 1956, 12.

11. Any administrative practice designed to move the student through school more rapidly than usual. Includes such practices as early admission, grade-skipping, advanced placement, telescoping of grade levels, credit by examination, etc.

SREB, 1962, 29.

ACCELERATION, ADAPTIVE: (See Adaptive Acceleration.)

ACCELERATION, INSTRUCTIONAL: (See Instructional Acceleration.)

ACCELERATION PROGRAM

A program which makes possible pupil attainment of a given educational level in a shorter time or at an earlier age than is normally expected.

Sumoption& Leucking, 1960, 63.

ACCELERATION, RADICAL: (See Radical Acceleration.)

ACCELERATION, SELECTIVE: (See Selective Acceleration.)

ACE: (See Accelerated College Enrollment Program.)

ACHIEVEMENT

(a) Accomplishment or proficiency of performance in a given skill or body of knowledge (b) progress in school; theoretically different from intelligence but overlaps with it to a degree.

Good, 1973, 7.

ACHIEVEMENT MOTIVATION

1. An hypothesized need to excel in achievement related situations (i.e. business, school).

Owen, Blount & Moscow, 1978, 544.

2. A combination of psychological forces which initiate, direct, and sustain behavior toward successful attainment of some goal which provides a sense of significance. No single measurable factor seems to account for it; measurement is in terms of construct validation of interrelated scholastic, societal, and individual factors.

Good, 1973, 375.

ACHIEVEMENT TEST

1. Any test that has a representative sampling of the course

content (that is possesses content validity) and that is designed to measure the extent of present knowledge . . . regardless of whether this test was constructed by the classroom teacher or by professional test makers. The major (but not the only) distinction between the standardized achievement test and the teacher-made test is that in a standardized achievement test, the systematic sampling of performance (that is, the pupil's score) has been obtained under prescribed directions of administration. They also differ markedly in terms of their sampling of content, construction, norms, and purpose and use.

Mehrens & Lehman, 1969, 133.

2. A test that measures the extent to which a person has "achieved" something, acquired certain information or mastered certain skills, usually as a result of specific instruction.

Hopke, 1968, 6.

3. A test designed to measure a person's knowledges, skills, understandings, etc. in a given field taught in school, for example, a mathematics test or an English test.

Good, 1973, 594.

4. A test designed to measure formal or "school-taught" learning.

Sax, 1980, 617.

ACHIEVER, LATENT; (See Latent Achiever).

ACTIVATING FACTOR

A factor described by Brandwein as being important to the successful scientist. This factor is concerned with opportunities for advanced training and contact with an inspirational teacher.

Brandwein, 1955, 11.

ADAPTIVE ACCELERATION

A term used to denote a teacher's letting a child in her class to do learning in her classroom which is associated with that of a higher grade level.

Newland, 1976, 258.

ADMISSION, EARLY: (See Early Admission).

ADVANCED PLACEMENT

1. Is a means whereby a high school student can gain college credit and/or advanced placement. Advanced standing is obtained by taking college level courses and/or an examination.

Fliegler, 1961, 27.

2. The status accorded to a student who is admitted to an

institution of higher education with educational attainment credited to him beyond the minimum required for admission; usually shortens the time necessary to complete diploma or degree requirements. Syn. Advanced Standing.
Good, 1973, 424.
3. Allowing bright students to demonstrate competency in required areas by means of testing or review of credentials.
Suran & Rizzo, 1979, 487.

ADVANCED PLACEMENT PROGRAM
1. A program, adopted in 1956, under which high school students can gain college credit for special courses; a national committee provides course descriptions and consultative service to participating high schools and grades the special examinations required by colleges for placement and credit. Syn. Advanced Standing.
Good, 1973, 442.
2. Through the Advanced Placement Program coordinated by the College Entrance Examination Board, college level courses may be taught in high schools as a way of challenging and accelerating superior students. Content is influenced by suggested criteria and syllabi as well as by the nature of the CEEB examinations. Essay questions predominate and are aimed at measuring the quality of thinking rather than mastery of facts alone.
Syphers, 1972, 20-21.

AFFECTIVE DEVELOPMENT
Development that involves awareness, receiving, responding, valuing, and integration into a value structure.
Clark, 1979, 178.

AFFECTIVE LEARNING
Consists of responses (expressed as positive or negative feelings) acquired as one evaluates the meaning of an idea, object, person, or event in terms of the maintenance and enhancement of his view of himself and the world.
Perkins, 1974, 571.

AP: (See Advanced Placement)

APT: Academic Promise Test (See Appendix D).

APTITUDE
1. (a) A group of characteristics deemed to be symptomatic of an individual's ability to acquire proficiency in a given area; examples might be a particular art, school subject, or

vocational area; (b) ability measured by the amount of time required by the learner to acquire mastery of a task; thus, given enough time, all students can conceivably attain such mastery.
Good, 1973, 39.
2. A natural tendency or an acquired inclination in some specific direction.
Sumption & Leucking, 1960, 58.
3. Readiness for learning. This readiness depends, in unknown proportions, on the genetic characteristics of the individual and his whole life history of physical surroundings and previous learnings.
Thorndike, 1969, 649.
4. Specific behavioral efficiencies, usually accompanied by above average general intelligence. These special abilities may be inferred through superior performance in subject areas such as mathematics and foreign languages, in skilled interpersonal relations which make for social leadership, in various forms of artistic expression such as music, dance or painting, and in still other particular kinds of behavior.
SREB, 1962, 26.

APTITUDE TEST
1. A cognitive test designed to predict achievement prior to instruction or selection.
Sax, 1980, 617.
2. A device used to assess a combination of native and acquired abilities, which are considered indicative of future performance.
Good, 1973, 595.

ARTICULATION OF GIFTED PROGRAMS
The sequential arrangements of studies through the total school program so as to avoid undesirable repetition or duplication at various grade levels. Problems of articulation often arise when programs for the gifted are planned to affect given school years but not to encompass entire graded sequence.
SREB, 1962, 29.

ASSESSMENT
The process by which as many data as possible are gathered and used to evaluate a person more accurately.
Good, 1973, 43.

ASSESSMENT, PROCESS: (See Process Assessment).

ASSOCIATION FOR THE GIFTED, THE (TAG):(See Appendix B).

ATTRIBUTE LISTING
A technique that promotes a clearer view of the qualities, specifications, characteristics, limitations, and attributes of a problem to allow for easy change and the development of new ideas through the change.
Feldhusen & Treffinger, 1977, 40.

AUDIENCE
The others present during the psychodrama. The audience may be the psychotherapy group, a seminar or class in school, other members of the protagonist's family. (See Psychodrama).
Blatner, 1973, 7.

AUTONOMOUS PERSON
The person who is liberated from rigid adherence to parental values or to social pressures and expectancies. He flexibly applies his values and principles in order to behave in ways appropriate to the situations he is in.
Johnson, 1972, 3.

AUXILIARY EGO
Also called auxiliary. The term for anyone besides the protagonist and the director who takes part in a psychodrama. (See Psychodrama).
Blatner, 1973, 6.

B

BALDWIN IDENTIFICATION MATRIX (BIM)
Baldwin Identification Matrix Inservice Kit for the Identification of Gifted and Talented Students. A systematic, versatile approach to identifying gifted and talented students in any student population. A matrix design that assists in the pulling together of all assessment techniques into a profile which allows a child equal access to a specifically designed program for children who exhibit exceptional ability in a wide range of areas.
Baldwin & Wooster, 1977.

BEH: (See Bureau of Education for the Handicapped)

BEHAVIORAL IDENTIFICATION OF GIFTEDNESS
A questionnaire developed by Charlotte Malone (1974) for the purpose of identifying mentally gifted kindergarten children.
Malone, 1975, 163.

BEHAVIORAL SOI
Information essentially non-verbal, involved in human interactions where the attitudes, needs, desires, moods, intentions, perceptions, thoughts, etc., of other people and of ourselves are involved.
Meeker, 1969, 196.

BIG: (See Behavioral Identification of Giftedness)

BILINGUAL
Having equal facility in the use of two languages.
Good, 1973, 62.

BLOOM'S TAXONOMY:
A taxonomy that gives a hierarchy of cognitive behaviors, and sample objectives for each level of the hierarchy. See also cognitive domain.
Owen, Blount, & Moscow 1978, 545.

BRAINSTORMING
1. A strategy which allows groups to explore ideas without judgment or censor, its rationale is that a greater fluency of ideas is believed to produce ideas of higher quality.
Clark, 1979, 202.
2. A popular non-technical term for certain techniques for the stimulation of creative thinking in the development of new

ideas; consists of individual or, more generally, small-group activity in which a deliberate attempt is made to think uncritically but creatively about all possible approaches and solutions to a given problem, the group participating in spontaneous and unrestrained discussion which usually involves evaluative feedback.

Good, 1973, 70.

3. A procedure meant to enhance creative thinking in groups. A problem is presented and the group generates many possible solutions; evaluation of solutions is deferred until a later time.

Owen, Blount, & Moscow 1978, 545.

4. A technique used to produce ideas related to a particular problem, topic, or theme. It is an excellent technique for strengthening imagination, flexibility, and discussion techniques. It is also a highly successful tool for problem solving that can be conveniently used in nearly every subject area and situation.

Feldhusen, & Treffinger, 1977, 39.

BRIGHT

Well above the norm in mental capacity and academic achievement.

Good, 1973, 71.

BRIGHT CHILD

(1) A child who is above the average in intellectual ability:
(2) A child who learns relatively easily.

Good, 1973, 94.

BUREAU OF EDUCATION FOR THE HANDICAPPED

The target population is children and youth who are gifted and talented, learning disabled, hearing impaired, visually impaired, and physically handicapped; those who have behavioral disorders; teacher training programs and early childhood programs. The Bureau of Education for the Handicapped is responsible for the administration of federal programs for the gifted and talented (P.L. 93-380, Section 404) and the Handicapped (P.L. 94-142). It also provides information regarding existing programs, persons to contact, current projects being funded, future funding opportunities, and agencies and organizations which could provide further assistance.

Maker, 1977, 137.

C

CAI MODEL: (See Cognitive-Affective Behaviors in the Classroom Model)

CALIFORNIA TEST OF MENTAL MATURITY: (See Appendix D)

CAPABILITY
The ultimate limit of an individual's possible development as determined at a given time, assuming optimum environment and training from that time onward.
Good, 1973, 78.

CAPACITY
1. (A term which means) potential ability. The ultimate limits to which an individual could develop any function given optimum training and environment.
Hopke, 1968, 51.
2. The ultimate limit to which an individual could develop any function, given optimum training and environment.
Good, 1973, 78.

CAPACITY FOR LEARNING
Accurate perception of social and matural situations; independent, rapid, efficient learning of fact and principle; fast meaningful readings, with superior retention and recall. (Educationally significant behavior of gifted students).
SREB, 1962, 23.

CAPACITY, LEARNING
The power of receiving and retaining concepts, data, and skills; the comprehensiveness or receptiveness of the mind; more generally, the potential, determined by heredity and environment, for latent change in or actual overt modification of the behavior of an organism.
Good, 1973, 78.

CAPACITY, MENTAL
A generally determined maximum level of potential performance of the mind, as contrasted with ability which describes the current level of mental achievement.
Good, 1973, 78.

CAREER EXPLORATION
Investigative activities or inquiries undertaken inside and outside the classroom to search out the necessary information

about a future occupational or professional interest or goal.
Good, 1973, 80.

CBC

Cognition of behavioral classes. The ability to see similarity of behavioral information in different expressional modes.
Meeker, 1969, 47.

CBI

Cognition of behavioral implications. The ability to draw implications or make predictions about what will happen following a given social situation.
Meeker, 1969, 49.

CBR

Cognition of behavioral relations. The ability to understand social relationships.
Meeker, 1969, 47.

CBS

Cognition of behavioral systems. The ability to comprehend a social situation or sequence of social events.
Meeker, 1969, 47.

CBT

Cognition of behavioral transformation. The ability to reinterpret either a gesture, a facial expression, a statement, or a whole situation so that its behavioral significance is changed.
Meeker, 1969, 48.

CBU

Cognition of behavioral units. The ability to understand units of expression, such as facial expression.
Meeker, 1969, 46.

CEC: (See Council for Exceptional Children; Appendix B).

CEILING

The upper limit of ability that can be measured by a test. Individuals are said to have reached the ceiling of a test when they have abilities that are above the highest performance level at which the test can make reliable discriminations. When the ceiling of a test is reached with an individual or group, the next higher level of the test should be used.
Robb, Bernardoni, & Johnson, 1972, 333.

CEILING AGE
>The age level on an intelligence test at which the individual misses or fails all items.
>>Sax, 1980, 618.

CFC
>Cognition of figural classes. The ability to recognize classes of figural items of information.
>>Meeker, 1969, 32.

CFI
>Cognition of figural implications. The ability to foresee the consequences involved in figural problems.
>>Meeker, 1969, 36.

CFR
>Cognition of figural relations.   The ability to recognize figural relations between forms.
>>Meeker, 1969, 33.

CFS
>Cognition of figural systems.   The ability to comprehend arrangements and positions of visual objects in space.
>>Meeker, 1969, 34.

CFT
>Cognition of figural transformations. The ability to visualize how a given figure or object will appear after given changes, such as unfolding or rotations.
>>Meeker, 1969, 35.

CFU-A
>Cognition of figural units—auditory. The ability to perceive auditory figural units (sounds) by organizing groups of successive inputs.
>>Meeker, 1969, 31.

CFU-V
>Cognition of figural units—visual. The ability to recognize a figural entity, that is, to "close" figural information or perceive a complete visual form.
>>Meeker, 1969, 30.

CHECKLIST
>A type of rating scale containing items that are checked or left

Checklist 16

blank depending on whether some aspect of behavior has been observed or not. (See Rating Scale).
Sax, 1980, 618.

CHILD, ACADEMICALLY TALENTED
A child who can be expected to attend college and benefit from enriched experiences in high school as well as college; a term used first by the Conference on the Academically Talented.
Good, 1973, 94.

CHILD, ACCELERATED
1. A child who has negotiated the school grades more rapidly than one grade per year; syn. accelerated pupil.
2. A child whose achievements or mental growth is beyond that of the average child of the same chronological age.
Good, 1973, 94.

CHILD, MINORITY GROUP: (See Minority Group Child)

CHILD, PRECOCIOUS: (See Precocious Child)

CHILD, PSEUDO-GIFTED: (See Pseudo-gifted Child)

CHILD, SUPERIOR; (See Superior Child)

CHRONIC UNDERACHIEVER
(A child whose pattern of underachievement) reoccurs again and again presenting a problem particularly resistant to remediation.
Clark, 1979, 279.

CHRONOLOGICAL AGE
Age computed from one's date of birth, used as the denominator in many quotient norms.
Sax, 1980, 618.

CLASS, HOMOGENEOUS SPECIAL
A class organized with the intent of containing a group of children possessing maximum similarity on one particular dimension or attribute in order to provide appropriate instruction focused on that attribute; in practice usually recognized as falling short of the content.
Good, 1973, 101.

CLASS, HONORS: (See Honors Class).

CLASSES, SOI
Conceptions underlying sets of items of information grouped by virtue of their common properties.
Meeker, 1969, 196.

CMC
Cognition of semantic classes. The ability to recognize common properties of words, ideas, and objects.
Meeker, 1969, 43.

CMI
Cognition of semantic implications. The ability to anticipate or be sensitive to the needs of or the consequences of a given situation in meaningful terms.
Meeker, 1969, 45.

CMR
Cognition of semantic relations. The ability to see relations between ideas or meanings of words.
Meeker, 1969, 43.

CMS
Cognition of semantic systems. The ability to comprehend relatively complex ideas.
Meeker, 1969, 44.

CMT
Cognition of semantic transformation. The ability to see potential changes of interpretations of objects and situations.
Meeker, 1969, 44.

CMU
Cognition of semantic units. The ability to comprehend the meanings of words or ideas.
Meeker, 1969, 41.

COGNITION
1. In general, the process of knowing; in particular, the process of knowing based upon perception, introspection, or memory.
Good, 1973, 113.
2. Involves the act of structuring information.
Guilford, 1977, 72.
3. Immediate discovery, awareness, rediscovery, or recognition of information in various forms, comprehension or understanding.
Meeker, 1969, 195.

4. Thinking and learning; the study of cognition focuses as how humans and other organisms acquire, organize, store, and use information.
Owen, Blount, Moscow, 1978, 546.
5. Refers to all the intellective activities of the mind, such as thinking, knowing, remembering, perceiving, recognizing, or generalizing.
Pulaski, 1971, 224.

COGNITIVE-AFFECTIVE BEHAVIORS IN THE CLASSROOM MODEL
A three dimensional model designed to aid teachers in modifying tasks in the classroom along the dimensions of curriculum, pupil behavior, and teacher behavior.
Williams, 1970, 203.

COGNITIVE DEVELOPMENT
1. Rests on the analysis, integration, and evaluation of a vast quantity of experiences of the environment and on an understanding of those experiences.
Clark, 1979, 162.
2. The acquisition of thinking skills and intelligence. Development results from the interaction of genetic potential and environmental experiences, and is thought to occur in a naturally unfolding sequence.
Owen, Blount, Moscow, 1978, 546.

COGNITIVE DOMAIN
The area of human behavior that involves thinking, knowing, understanding, and comprehending.
Owen, Blount, Moscow, 1978, 546.

COGNITIVE PROCESSES
The processes through which one acquires, organizes, interrelates, and interprets the data of his experience. Cognitive processes include labeling, forming hypotheses, evaluating, and applying rules of transformation.
Perkins, 1974, 527.

COMMUNICATION
The act of a person sending a message to another individual with the conscious intent of evoking a response. The message may be a verbal, nonverbal, or behavioral stimulus that the sender transmits to the receiver. (See also Effective Communication).
Johnson, 1972, 61.

CONTENTS, SOI
Broad classes or types of information discriminable by the organism.
Meeker, 1969, 195.

CONVERGENT CREATIVITY
This is the kind of creativity that is, called forth by our best examination when they require the bringing together of ideas from many sources in order to answer the test question. At its best, this demand does stimulate the reorganization of concepts.
Reissman, 1962, 79.

CONVERGENT PRODUCTION
1. The other kind of productive thinking. It also is concerned with retrieval of items of information from memory storage for use in answering questions and solving problems. Whereas in divergent production a number of alternative answers are wanted and will do, in convergent production only one answer will ordinarily satisfy the requirements of the question or problem. Only one answer is considered correct.
Guilford, 1977, 109.
2. Generation of information from given information, where the emphasis is upon achieving unique or conventionally accepted best outcomes. It is likely that the given information (cue) fully determines the response.
Meeker, 1969. 195.

CONVERGENT THINKING
1. Convergent thinking refers to the process whereby the student takes a large number of facts or associations, and puts them together in certain predictable combinations to come out with the one right possible answer. The clearest academic illustrations of convergent thinking can be found in arithmetic reasoning problems, where the student takes a variety of facts and pulls them together to come out with the right answer. All instances of deductive reasoning involve convergent thinking.
Gallagher, 1975, 239.
2. A type of thinking appropriate for closed-solution-type (one answer) problems whereby the individual attempts to operate according to prescribed and tested forms of analysis, method, and judgment.
Good, 1973, 608.

COURSE, HONORS: (See Honors Course)

CREATION
   The combination of items of fact or experience by the mechanism
   of the subconscious in a relation which satisfies an existing
   concept of livingness.
                    Austin, 1925, 16.

CREATIVE ABILITY, SCIENTIFIC :   (See Scientific Creative
Ability)

CREATIVE LEARNING PROCESS
   A process of becoming sensitive to or aware of problems,
   deficiencies, gaps in knowledge, missing elements, disharmonies,
   and so on; bringing together available information; defining the
   difficulty or identifying the missing elements, searching for
   solutions, making guesses, or formulating hypotheses about the
   deficiencies; testing and retesting them; perfecting; and
   finally communicating the results.
                    Torrance & Myers, 1970, 22

CREATIVELY GIFTED
   Individuals who exhibit superior ability in creative or
   productive thinking often are referred to as creatively gifted
   ... their ability to think divergently and develop new, unique,
   and   original   ideas   sets   them   apart   in   this   category.
                    Martinson, 1974, 474.

CREATIVENESS
   The   desire . and   the   power   to   make   something   new.
                    Hall, 1956, 32.

CREATIVE POSITIVES
   A set of characteristics that help to guide the search for the
   strengths of culturally different students and for giftedness
   among   such   students.
                    Torrance, 1973, 5-8.

CREATIVE PROCESS
   The emergence in action of a novel relational product, growing
   out of the uniqueness of the individual on the one hand and the
   materials, events, people, or circumstances of his life on the
   other.
                    Rogers, 1954, 71.

CREATIVE THINKING
   1. In creative thinking the individual strives to discover new
   solutions to problems, to see new relationships, or to find new

modes of artistic expression. He tries to discover new and better ways of achieving goals. His thinking brings into existence something which is new for society, or at least for himself.

Engle, 1964, 120.

2. . . . the "imaginatively gifted recombination of known elements into something new."

Osborn, 1967, 478.

3. Creative thinking will be used to refer to such abilities as fluency (large number of ideas), flexibility (variety of different approaches or categories of ideas), originality (unusual, off the beaten path ideas), elaboration (well developed and detailed ideas), sensitivity to defects established, or intended way or use.

Torrance, 1965, 4.

4. Consists of mental processes that cause children to reach out and go beyond what they know. Such processes deal with unknowns by thinking about things that have not happened or things that might be. When this kind of thinking takes place, different associations are formed among known facts which now fit into some new pattern. Such relationships may not necessarily be new to the world nor mankind, but will be at least new and occur for the first time to the child who creates.

Williams, 1972, 29.

5. Thinking that is inventive, that explores novel situations, that teaches new solutions to old problems, or that results in thoughts original with the thinker.

Good, 1973, 608.

CREATIVELY HANDICAPPED

Children whose behavior problems stem from the differences their abilities create between them and other children and between them and their teachers. Their learning difficulties arise from the incompatibility between their abilities and learning preferences on one hand and the teaching methods and system of rewards of the school on the other.

Gowan & Torrance, 1971, 212-213.

CREATIVITY

1. The human attribute of constructive originality; many include such factors as associative and educational fluency, adaptive and spontaneous flexibility, and ability to elaborate in detail; may be fostered or inhibited by teaching procedures; operationally defined by specific productions such as inventions, paintings, discovery of principles, etc. or by standardized tests. Beyond a fairly low minimum level does not

appear to correlate either positively or negatively with intelligence.

Good, 1973, 152.

2. The capacity of persons to produce compositions, products, or ideas of any sort which are essentially new or novel, and previously unknown to the producer. It can be imaginative activity, or thought synthesis, where the product is no mere summation. It may involve the forming of new patterns and combinations of information derived from past experience, and the transplanting of old relationships to new situations, and may involve the generation of new correlates. It must be purposeful or goal directed, not mere old fantasy—although it need not have immediate practical application or be a perfect and complete product. It may take the form of an artistic, literary or scientific production or may be a procedural or methodological nature.

Drevdahl, 1956, 22.

3. The ability to bring something new into existence . . . Since human beings are not able to make something out of nothing, the human act of creation always involves a reshaping of given materials whether physical or mental. The 'something new' is a form made by the reconstitution of, or regeneration from something old.

Gallagher, 1975, 239.

4. ...is conceptualized as part of intellectual functioning (and as such it is distinct from intelligence only as intelligence has been operationalized and measured in standard aptitude tests). It is part of intelligence, but a part that is not measured by the conventional intelligence test.

Guilford, 1967, 288.

5. A way of conducting one's life rather than in terms of the number and kinds of objects which one may have produced.

Hallman, 1963, 132.

6. A cognitive ability usually given special importance in school, although it is difficult to separate from IQ & to measure. Most measures of creativity stress the number, variety, & especially originality of ideas that people are able to generate in response to particular situations.

Hurlock, 1957, 420.

7. A complex process that usually involves a range of qualities including awareness, originality, fluency, flexibility, commitment, and complexity.

Leeper & Skipper, 1974, 351.

8. A process extended in time and characterized by originality, adaptiveness and realization. It may be brief, as in musical improvisation, or it may involve a considerable span of years as

was required for Darwin's creation of the theory of evolution. It fulfills at least three conditions:

a. It involves a response or an idea that is novel or at least statistically infrequent.

b. It must to some extent be adaptive to, or of reality. It must serve to solve a problem, fit a situation, or accomplish some recognizable goal.

c. True creativeness involves a sustaining of the original insight, an evaluation and elaboration of it, a developing of it to the full.

MacKinnon, 1962, 484-495.

9. Something new into birth . . . the expression of the normal man in the art of actualizing himself . . . as the representation of the highest degree of emotional health.

May, 1959, 57, 58.

10. The production of a unique or novel response to a problem. Most definitions, but not all, include the requirement that the unique response be culturally useful.

Owen, Blount & Moscow, 1978, 547.

11. A function of knowledge, imagination, and evaluation. The process involved as fact finding, problem finding, idea finding, solution finding, and acceptance finding.

Parnes, 1967, 246.

12. An arbitrary harmony, an expected astonishment, a habitual revelation, a familiar surprise, a generous selfishness, an unexpected certainty, a formable stubbornness, a vital triviality, a disciplined freedom, an intoxicating steadiness, a repeated initiation, a difficult delight, a predictable gamble, an ephemereal solidity, a unifying difference, a demanding satisfier, a miraculous expectation, an accustomed amazement.

Prince, 1970, xiii.

13. The birth of an idea and its embodiment in form recognizable by someone or society as valuable.

Rhodes, 1963, 305

14. The capacity to restructure the world in unusual conceptual terms.

Suran & Rizzo, 1979, 488.

CREATIVITY, CONVERGENT: (See Convergent Creativity)

CREATIVITY, EMERGENTIVE: (See Emergentive Creativity)

CREATIVITY, EXPRESSIVE: (See Expressive Creativity)

CREATIVITY, INNOVATIVE: (See Innovative Creativity)

CREATIVITY, INVENTIVE: (See Inventive Creativity)

CREATVITY, PRODUCTIVE: (See Productive Creativity)

CREATIVITY TEST
A measure of novel or divergent thinking.
> Sax, 1980, 619.

CRITERION REFERENCED TESTS
1. Tests of specific content skills, teacher written or published. These measures have a predetermined standard or criteria of performance against which the student is compared.
> Clark, 1979, 123.

2. A test designed to measure content as specified by behavioral objectives; generally any test having a specified minimal level of attainment and not designed to measure individual differences.
> Sax, 1980, 619.

CRITICAL THINKING
1. The process of examining both concrete and verbal materials in the light of related objective evidence comparing the object or statement with some norm or standard, and concluding or acting upon the judgment then made.
> Russell, 1956, 285.

2. The productive thinking ability that enables us to solve problems, plan and implement ideas and activities, and handle life without a floor plan or set of directions. It should be the most important phenomenon of learning for a teacher to develop, and it definitely is a creative, productive activity.
> Feldhusen & Treffinger, 1977, 38.

3. Thinking that proceeds on the basis of careful evaluation of premises and evidence and comes to conclusions as objectively as possible through the consideration of all pertinent factors and the use of valid procedures from logic.
> Good, 1973, 608.

CROSS-AGE TUTORING: (See Peer Tutoring)

CSC
Cognition of symbolic classes. The ability to recognize common properties in sets of symbolic information.
> Meeker, 1969, 38.

CSI
Cognition of symbolic implications. The ability to foresee or

to be sensitive to consequences in a symbolic problem.
Meeker, 1969, 40.

CSR

Cognition of symbolic relations. The ability to see relations
between items of symbolic information.
Meeker, 1969, 39.

CSS

Cognition of symbolic systems. The ability to understand the
systematic interrelatedness of symbols within an organized set.
Meeker, 1969, 39.

CSU-A

Cognition of symbolic units—auditory. An auditory ability to
decode auditory information in the form of language symbols.
Meeker, 1969, 38.

CSU-V

Cognition of symbolic units—visual. A visual ability to
recognize graphic symbolic units such as words.
Meeker, 1969, 37.

CTMM: California Test of Mental Maturity (See Appendix D).

CULTURALLY DEPRIVED

Refers to those aspects of middle-class culture such as
education, books, formal language, from which these groups have
not benefited. He uses "culturally deprived" interchangeably
with "educationally deprived" to refer to the members of lower
socio-economic groups who have had limited access to education.
Reissman, 1962, 3.

CULTURALLY DIFFERENT

1. Means to be behaviorally different in group-identifiable
ways.
Bernal, 1976, 67.
2. Those cultural or sub-cultural groups whose cultural
environment differs from that of the mainstream or general
culture.
Bruch, 1975, 164.

CULTURALLY DIFFERENT GIFTED

1. Students are those who fall outside the mainstream of
society's dominant culture and may include Native American,
black, Chicano, female, rural, urban, or handicapped students.
Correll, 1978, 21.

2. The culturally different comprise one segment of a larger subpopulation called the educationally disadvantaged. This latter, broader group includes not only the culturally different but also the economically deprived, female, handicapped, rural, and underachieving. Thus, the major qualification in the definition of the culturally different is membership in a culture other than the dominant culture in society.
Sato, 1974, 573.

CULTURALLY DIFFERENT LEARNERS
Any student whose rearing is more typical of a culture that differs significantly in values and attitudes from the dominant culture. These students have unique problems even when not reared in conditions of poverty.
Clark, 1979, 287.

CULTURAL DIVERSITY
A condition of racial, ethnic, language, or physical differences from a dominant culture.
Baldwin, 1978, 1.

CULTURE
Includes goals or values that are states or conditions toward which we are obliged to strive.
Gottlieb & Ramsey, 1967, 5.

CULTURE-FAIR TEST
1. A measuring device that shows no inherent bias against or in favor of any particular ethnic, racial, or cultural group. Culture-fair tests are non existant, and appear to be impossible.
Owen, Blount, Moscow, 1978, 548.
2. A test that does not overselect or underselect members of various groups when they would have performed equally well on a criterion.
Sax, 1980, 619.

CULTURE-FREE TEST
A test that is free of the impact of all cultural experiences; therefore, a measure reflecting only hereditary abilities. Since culture permeates all of man's environmental contacts, the construction of such a test would seem to be an impossibility. Cultural "bias" is not eliminated by the use of nonlanguage or so-called performance tests, although it may be reduced in some instances. In terms of most of the purposes for which tests are

used, the validity (value) of "culture-free" test is questioned; a test designed to be equally applicable to all cultures may be of little or no practical value in any.

Mehrens & Lehmann, 1978, 692.

CUTTING SCORE

A test score used to separate persons selected from those rejected. High cutting scores help select more highly qualified persons but reduce the number of persons given a chance to succeed.

Sax, 1980, 619.

D

DEPRIVATION
A term implying a value judgment. It implies that various individuals or groups are hindered—some more, some less—in competing for certain valued ends of society.
Gottlieb & Ramsey, 1967, 5.

DESDEG: (See Diagnostic and Evaluative Scales for Differential Education for the Gifted)

DEVELOPMENTAL TASKS
Tasks that all individuals within a given society encounter as they progress from infancy to adulthood.
Perkins, 1974, 305.

DEVIATION IQ
1. A standard score used to express intelligence test performance usually with a mean of 100 and a standard deviation of 15 points. Computed by converting all scores to z scores, multiplying by 15, and adding 100.
Sax, 1980, 620.
2. A measure of intelligence based on the extent to which an individual's score deviates from a score that is normal for the individual's age.
Robb, Bernardoni, & Johnson, 1972, 335.

DFC
Divergent production of a figural classification. The ability to group figural information in different ways.
Meeker, 1969, 88.

DFI
Divergent production of figural implications. The ability to elaborate on figural information.
Meeker, 1969, 91.

DFS
Divergent production of a figural system. The ability to produce composites of figural information in many ways.
Meeker, 1969, 89.

DFT
Divergent production of a figural transformation. The ability to process figural information in revised ways.
Meeker, 1969, 87.

DIAGNOSTIC AND EVALUATIVE SCALES FOR
DIFFERENTIAL EDUCATION FOR THE GIFTED (DESDEG)
by Renzulli and Ward (1969)
A model developed as a guide for both self-study and for
assessment by an external evaluation team. The model represents
an attempt to bridge the gap between theory and practice in the
field of evaluation as it applies to programs for the gifted.
Although DESDEG was designed mainly for purpose of program
evaluation, the authors suggest that it can also be used as a
guide for program planning and development. The DESDEG model
consists of five interrelated components: (a) philosophy and
objectives, (b) student identification and placement, (c) the
curriculum, (d) the teacher, and (e) program organization and
operation.
Renzulli, 1975, 27.

DIAGNOSTIC TEST
1. A test used to point out specific strengths and weaknesses
of individuals. Standardized diagnostic tests are available in
mathematics and reading.
Sax, 1980, 620.
2. A test used to "diagnose" or analyze; that is to locate an
individual's specific areas of weakness or strength, to
determine the nature of his weaknesses or deficiencies, and,
wherever possible, to suggest their cause. Such a test yields
measures of the components of subparts of some larger body of
information or skill. Diagnostic achievement tests are most
commonly prepared for the skill subjects.
Mehrens & Lehmann, 1978, 693.

DIRECTOR
The person who guides the protagonist in the use of the
psychodramatic method in order to help the protagonist explore
his problem. (See Psychodrama).
Blatner, 1973, 6.

DISADVANTAGED
1. Being reared by poor, lower-class, native parents out of the
cultural mainstream.
Gowan, 1969, 240.
2. A term to denote those segments of our society whose style
of life is discernibly less nurturant to conventional learning
than the average of the total society. Most commonly, they are
found in the lower socioeconomic groups and constitute
relatively intact subgroups, such as certain white mountain

folk, the Blacks, the Puerto Ricans, the American Indians, and those of Mexican backgrounds, who have moved into the general culture of our country.

Newland, 1976, 47.

3. Refers primarily to the populations who are restricted in access to mainstream cultural experiences due to economic disadvantagement.

Bruch, 1975, 164.

DISADVANTAGED GIFTED

Those who, by reason of cultural or social disadvantages, have not had the opportunity for a broad range of intellectual, aesthetic, and cultural development may be deemed to be handicapped by less fulfulling experience. Such disadvantages are often associated with the diminished opportunities available to the poor, but may be present in any cultural group which has restricted possibilities to meet in the activities permitted to the general culture, learn and develop.

Gowan & Bruch, 1971, 76.

DISCOVERY LEARNING

An instructional process placing greater responsibility on the learner for finding information or problem solutions. Types of discovery learning range from leaving the student almost entirely on his or her own—called unguided discovery—to a more cooperative relationship, or guided discovery.

Owen, Blount & Moscow, 1978, 548.

DIVERGENT PRODUCTION

The development of more than one possible response to a problem or question. Believed to be a central characteristic of creativity.

Owen, Blount & Moscow, 1978, 549.

DIVERGENT PRODUCTION (SOI)

Generation of information from given information, where the emphasis is on variety and quantity of output from the same source. Likely to involve what has been called transfer. This operation is most clearly involved in aptitudes of creative potential.

Meeker, 1969, 195.

DIVERGENT THINKING

1. A much more free and open type of intellectual operation, in which the distinguishing characteristic is the large number of

possible associations or problem solutions.
Gallagher, 1975, 239.
2. Mental activity directed to open-end kinds of problems for which there is no one correct answer; the more infrequent statistically a response is under these conditions, the more divergent is the thinking.
Good, 1973, 608.

DMC

Divergent production of semantic classes. The ability to produce many categories of ideas appropriate in meaning to a given idea.
Meeker, 1969, 96.

DMI

Divergent production of semantic implications. The ability to produce many antecedents, concurrents or consequents of given information.
Meeker, 1969, 98

DMR

Divergent production of semantic relations. The ability to produce many relationships appropriate in meaning to a given idea.
Meeker, 1969, 97.

DMS

Divergent production of semantic systems. The ability to organize words in various meaningful complex ideas.
Meeker, 1969, 97.

DMT

Divergent production of semantic transformation. The ability to produce unusual, remote, or clever responses involving reinterpretations or new emphasis on some aspect of an object or situation.
Meeker, 1969, 98.

DMU

Divergent production of semantic units. The ability to produce many elementary ideas appropriate to given requirements.
Meeker, 1969, 96.

DROPOUT

Any student who has been enrolled and fails to re-enroll (either voluntarily or unvoluntarily) for the succeeding term or year

(usually excessive of summer terms) and who has not completed the normal degree of certificate objective of the program or institution concerned.
Hopke, 1968, 119.

DSC

Divergent production of symbolic classifications. The ability to group items of symbolic information in different ways.
Meeker, 1969, 93.

DSI

Divergent production of symbolic implications. The ability to produce varied implications from given symbolic information.
Meeker, 1969, 95.

DSR

Divergent production of symbolic relations. The ability to relate letters or numbers in many different ways.
Meeker, 1969, 93.

DSS

Divergent production of a symbolic system. The ability to organize sets of symbolic information into different systemic arrangements.
Meeker, 1969, 94.

DSU

Divergent production of symbolic units. The ability to produce many symbolic units which conform to simple specification not involving meaning.
Meeker, 1969, 92.

E

EARLY ADMISSION
1. A provision whereby a student enters kindergarten or first grade before his chronological age group. The selection process for early admission adheres to a set of criteria, which generally includes intelligence, academic performance, social and emotional maturity, and parental attitudes.
Fliegler, 1961, 27.

2. (a) the practice of acceleration by enrolling mentally advanced children when they are below the minimum legally permitted school age; an administrative practice usually dependent upon the recommendation of a school psychologist; (b) school enrollment of a handicapped child at preschool age level.
Good, 1973, 15.

ECONOMICALLY DEPRIVED
The terms culturally deprived, culturally different or economically deprived are used generically to represent all those children born into environments that often predispose them to be constitutionally inferior, and reared in environments that are at once psychologically inferior and socially debilitating.
Adler, 1968, xi.

EDUCATIONALLY TALENTED
A term which has been used by many educators in preference to "gifted," perhaps because the latter was regarded as too restrictive, and in preference to "mentally superior," probably because of negative connotations regarding the children not so characterized. This term was taken to denote both those children who had achieved outstandingly and those whose actual achievements were not as great as the evidence of learning potential suggested they might be—the "underachievers."
Newland, 1976, 10.

EDUCATION FOR ALL HANDICAPPED CHILDREN ACT
1. A federal law that became effective September, 1978; it guarantees equal educational opportunity for handicapped students. A major feature of the law is that handicapped children must be placed in an educational setting that is the least restrictive environment. Other features are: the right to due process, which protects an individual from erroneous classification, capricious labeling, and denial of equal education; protection against discriminatory testing in

diagnoses; and the establishment of individualized educational programs.
> Owen, Blount, and Moscow, 1978, 549.

EFFECTIVE COMMUNICATION
A state that exists between two persons when the receiver interprets the sender's message in the same way the sender intended it. In effective communication the messages of the sender directly reflect his intentions and the interpretations by the receiver match the intentions of the sender.
> Johnson, 1972, 62.

EFU
Evaluation of a figural unit. The ability to judge units of figural information as being similar or different.
> Meeker, 1969, 63.

ELABORATION
1. Includes the embellishments, details, or complexity added to a basic idea.
> Meyen, 1978, 476.

2.   The ability to add details to a basic idea produced.
> Khatena, 1978, 25.

EMC
Evaluation of semantic classes.   The ability to judge applicability of class properties of semantic information.
> Meeker, 1969, 70.

EMERGENTIVE CREATIVITY
The ability to absorb the experiences which are commonly provided by the environment and from these conventional experiences to produce something entirely new.
> Taylor, 1960,

EMI
Evaluation of semantic implications. The ability to judge adequacy of a meaningful deduction.
> Meeker, 1969, 72.

EMS
Evaluation of semantic systems. The ability to judge the internal consistency of a complex of meaningful information.
> Meeker, 1969, 71.

EMT
>Evaluation of semantic transformation. The ability to judge which objects or ideas could best be transformed or redefined in order to meet new requirements.
>>Meeker, 1969, 69.

EMU
>Evaluation of semantic units. The ability to make judgments about the suitability or adequacy of ideas and word meanings in terms of meeting certain given criteria.
>>Meeker, 1969, 69.

ENRICHED PROGRAM
>For gifted students involves:
>>a) emphasis on the creative and the experimental;
>>b) emphasis on the skills of investigation and learning;
>>c) independent work, stressing initiative and originality;
>>d) high standards of accomplishment;
>>e) co-operative planning and activity that provides opportunity for leadership training and experience in social adjustment;
>>f) individual attention given by teacher to student;
>>g) first-hand experiences;
>>h) flexibility of organization and procedure;
>>i) extensive reading; and
>>j) concern with community responsibility.
>>>Havighurst, Stivers, and DeHaan, 1955, 75.

ENRICHMENT
>1. Those activities which are designed specifically for the gifted student. In this sense, the term denotes a method, regardless of the general administrative organization that determines the gifted student's placement into a group. The term "enrichment in a regular classroom" refers to administrative organization of placing gifted students into heterogeneous groups on the basis of assigned grade levels. This group assignment is usually random and does not depend on achievement, intelligence or similar factors which classify the student as gifted.
>>Durr, 1964, 116.
>2. A policy, not a plan. It embraces all the curricular adjustments made for gifted students. These include experiences in breadth and depth and those connected with grouping acceleration and individualization of instruction in heterogeneous classes.
>>Gowan, 1964, 138.

3.   The addition of disciplines or areas of learning not normally found in the regular curriculum. One may also find more difficult or in-depth material available on the typical curricular subjects.   It is generally used in traditional classrooms to meet the needs of advanced learners without having to separate them from the typical learners at their grade level.

Clark, 1979, 144.

4. Any experience that replaces, supplements, or extends instruction normally offered by the school.

Correll, 1978, 2.5.

5.   The substitution of beneficial learning for needless repetition and harmful idleness. The qualifying objectives are necessary because not everything that goes under the name of enrichment is beneficial, much drill may be necessary, and not all idleness is harmful.

Cutts & Mosely 1957, 37.

6. Refers to the arrangement whereby the classroom teacher differentiates the curriculum and teaching methods in accordance with the individual differences among his pupils so that they have maximum opportunity to develop their abilities.

DeHaan, 1963, 46.

7. Any modification of class instruction that provides more challenge for the gifted mind than regular classwork affords. It chiefly involves teaching how to learn and study independently with books and other materials that are available to them.   Enrichment explores topics outside the standard curriculum. Enrichment is most commonly thought of as parallel study for bright children on a more advanced level than that being done by the rest of the class. True enrichment occurs when pupils are challenged to undertake problem solving and original work beyond the interests and abilities of the rest of the class.

Hildreth, 1966, 212.

8. A supplement to regular school curriculum offerings that include honors courses, independent study programs, summer school programs, electives, and special co-curricular projects.

Walker, 1978, 489.

9. A special effort to challenge the abilities of gifted pupils in their experiences in and out of the classroom and consists of giving the gifted child the opportunity to go more deeply into things, to range more widely than the average child.

Laycock, 1967, 75.

10. The provision of learning opportunities for children in addition to the content of education. It at once becomes apparent that enrichment can refer to anything from the

passively informative to the penetrating or broadly exploratory.
Newland, 1976, 281.

11. The selection and organization of learning experiences appropriate to youths' adequate development. It is not, therefore, "special education" in the meaning in which the term is generally used—giving attention to students with unusual problems—but rather the essence of all good education.
Passow, 1958, 193.

12. A program planned to develop the potentialities of intellectually gifted students by arranging a learning environment conducive to exploration and originality; by considering individual differences; by including depth and scope in learning experiences; and by providing opportunities for reflective thinking, problem solving, critical thinking, and creative thinking. Enrichment is based on the characteristics of the learners, the needs of society, principles of learning, sociopsychological implications, levels of intellectual functioning, and the logic and sequence of subject-matter fields.
Plowman & Rice, 1969, 6.

13. Practices which are intended to increase the depth or breadth of the gifted student's learning experiences. May include special assignments, independent study, individual projects, small group work, and other adaptations of routine school processes. This purported form of provision for the gifted often in fact merely camouflages do-nothingness.
SREB, 1962, 30.

14. A way of giving better educational opportunities to the mentally advanced child. It implies providing experiences for which the average or below average child lacks either the time, the interest or the ability to understand.
Worcester, 1956, 39.

15. A policy rather than a plan; in a narrow sense, enrichment is often used to describe the deliberate differentiation of curriculum content and activities for the superior pupils in a heterogeneous class.
EPC, 1950, 55.

16. Learning experiences that will meet their needs and 'stretch' their abilities. It means a curriculum that is 'expanded' and that will provide a challenge. This does not imply any neglect of basic skills. It will consist not of adding more of the same content but of providing situations at a more advanced level to match the higher levels of gifted children.
DeHaan & Havighurst, 1961, 96.

17. More opportunities for the gifted child to go deeper and to

Enrichment 38

range more widely than the average child in his intellectual, social, and artistic experience.
DeHaan & Havighurst, 1961, 97.

18. Consists of learning experiences that are advanced, that require mental functions more complex than the average, that require greater than average speed at higher levels of generalization and abstraction, and that are designed with the needs and capabilities of particular students in mind.
DeHaan, 1960, 139.

19. The practice of providing additional kinds of learning experiences beyond those offered in the regular program.
Sumption & Leucking, 1960, 171.

20. The type of activity devoted to further development of the particular intellectual skills and talents of the gifted child. These might be described as:
1. The ability to associate and interrelate concepts.
2. The ability to evaluate facts and arguments critically.
3. The ability to create new ideas and originate new lines of thought.
4. The ability to reason through complex problems.
5. The ability to understand other situations, other times, and other people, to be less bound by one's own peculiar environment.
Gallagher, 1975, 76-77.

21. Experiences which replace, supplement, or extend learnings as the basis for such type of prototype.
Kaplan, 1977, 381.

ENRICHMENT MODEL, THE
Relying on the typical curriculum as a skeletal structure, the main thrust of enrichment programs is supplementation. The supplemental content may take one of two main forms: (1) additive knowledge which embellishes upon basic concepts (so-called horizontal enrichment) or (2) qualitatively different or advanced topics not ordinarily dealt with at a given grade level (so-called vertical enrichment). This model represents the only compromise between general and special education.
Rice, 1970, 290.

ESC
Evaluation of symbolic classes. The ability to judge applicability of class properties of symbolic information, that is, judging of a class in which to place numbers, letters or signs.
Meeker, 1969, 65.

ESI
Evaluation of symbolic implications. Describes the ability to judge whether there is consistency of, probability of, or inferences from given symbolic information.
Meeker, 1969, 68.

ESR
Evaluation of symbolic relations. The ability to make choices among symbolic relationships of similarity and consistency in given letters or numerals.
Meeker, 1969, 65.

ESS
Evaluation of symbolic systems. The ability to estimate appropriateness of aspect of a symbolic system.
Meeker, 1969, 66.

EST
Evaluation of symbolic transformation. The ability to judge whether or not an ordering of substitutive symbols is adequate.
Meeker, 1969, 67.

ESU
Evaluation of symbolic units. The ability to make rapid decisions regarding the identification of letter or number sets.
Meeker, 1969, 64

ETHICAL GIFTEDNESS
Refers to a moral person who characteristically:
a) Chooses the ethical rather than the expedient alternatives....
b) Stands against public sentiment...
c) Feels allegiance and responsibility for principles and causes...
d) Identifies with humanity...beyond his own group
e) Feels compassion for wrongdoers without condoning specific acts
f) Perceives and admits to his own shortcomings
g) Holds to personal ideas transcending...appearance and social acceptability
Gallagher, 1975, 16.

EVALUATION
1. The process of making decisions based on the results of measurements or observations. Evaluation strategies describe

the elements that go into this decision-making process.
Sax, 1980, 621.
2. The process of delineating, obtaining, and providing useful
information for judging decision alternatives.
Stufflebeam, 1971, xxv.

EVALUATION (SOI)
Reaching decisions or making judgments concerning criterion
satisfaction (correctness, suitability, adequacy, desirability,
etc.) of information.
Meeker, 1969, 195.

EVALUATION, FORMATIVE: (See Formative Evaluation)

EVALUATION, SUMMATIVE: (See Summative Evaluation)

EXCELLENCE
The fact or condition of excelling; superiority. Something in
which a person or thing excels, a particular virtue.
Webster, 1968, 261.

EXCEPTIONAL
1. Description of a pupil who displays a deviation from the
normal by a considerable amount in respect to any one of a
number of traits.
Good, 1973, 223.
2. An accepted technical term which is used for children who
deviate markedly from the average, whether physically,
intellectually, or socially.
Laycock, 1967, 9.
3. Refers to a child whose ability or performance deviates from
normal. While much attention goes to children with handicaps,
the gifted or talented youngster is also exceptional.
Owen, Blount and Moscow, 1978, 550.

EXCEPTIONAL CHILDREN
Includes all students who have extreme differences in mental or
physical functioning which prevent them from achieving their
best potential in a regular program and who therefore require
some special or supplemental instruction and services.
Hopke, 1968, 134-135.

EXPRESSIVE CREATIVITY
Independent expression in which skills, originality, and quality
are relatively unimportant.
Taylor, 1960, 8.

41 Extra Classroom Prototypes

EXTRA-CLASSROOM PROTOTYPES
Programs which function outside the boundaries of the regular classroom. They are the learning opportunities which exist as a supplemental unit to the regular classroom program. Kaplan, 1977, 54.

F

FAST-PACED MATHEMATICS
A special process developed by SMPY. It is a method or technique whereby a student is able to telescope his or her learning time of a particular mathematics sequence while interacting with intellectual peers in a rigorous classroom situation.
George, 1979, 120.

FEEDBACK
Self-disclosing about how you are reacting to the way another person is behaving.
Johnson, 1972, 15.

FIGURAL CONTENT
Concrete material such as is perceived through the senses. It does not represent anything except itself.
Guilford, 1959, 470.

FIGURAL (SOI)
Information in concrete form, as perceived or as recalled possibly in the form of images. The term "figural" minimally implies figure-ground perceptual organization. Visual spatial information is figural. Different sense modalities may be involved; e.g. visual kinesthetic.
Meeker, 1969, 195.

FIRST-ORDER GIFTED
Children in the upper one-tenth of 1 percent. (Also referred to as) extremely gifted children.
Havighurst, 1961, 528.

FLEXIBILITY
1. The ability to adapt to changing instructions, to be free of thought, to use a variety of approaches.
Torrance, 1963, 96.
2. The ability to produce ideas that show a person's movement from one level of thinking to another, or shifts in thinking relative to a given task. Ideas that do the same job do not show shifts in thinking.
Khatena, 1978, 25.

FLUENCY
1. a) The frequency with which ideas or symbols can be expressed in a given time.
b) A trait often found in creative people, but fluency without originality may not result in creative expression.
McFee, 1970, 163.
2. Refers to a number of ideas of a similar kind. The ideas of using bricks to build a house, to build a wall etc., are ideas in the same category...It means that the ideas should be within the boundary of an exclusive category. The category may be a requirement, a relation, or a connected discourse.
Kuo, 1976, 87.
3. Concerned primarily with efficient retrieval of many items of information that fulfill certain specifications. The individual examines many different kinds of items that are stored, and the wider the range of ideas called out of storage, the greater the fluency.
Wilson, Robeck, & Michael, 1967, 195.
4. The ability to produce many ideas for a given task.
Khatena, 1978, 24.

FORMATIVE EVALUATION
The use of tests to obtain feedback during the course of a program rather than at its termination point. Formative evaluation allows projects to be modified and improved upon while they are in progress.
Sax, 1980, 622.

FUNCTIONAL ASSESSMENT
Observations of a student working to determine level of functioning.
Clark, 1979, 123.

G

GENERALIZING
    The act of deriving a general concept, principle, law, or theory
    from particular facts of observations.
                Perkins, 1974, 538.

GENETIC FACTORS
    Factors observed by Brandwein as characteristics of those who
    remained in scientific research. The factors were high level
    verbal and mathematical ability, and adequate sensory and
    neuromuscular control.
                Brandwein, 1955, 9.

GENIUS
    1. Anyone who, regardless of other characteristics he may
    possess or have attributed to him, produces over a long period
    of time, a large body of work that has a significant influence
    on many persons for many years; requiring these people, as well
    as the individual in question, to come to terms with a different
    set of attitudes, ideas, viewpoints, or techniques before all
    can have "peace of mind", that is, a sense of resolution and
    closure. The key ingredient to genius is productivity—large in
    volume, extraordinary in longevity, more or less unpredictable
    in content.
                Albert, 1976, 316.
    2. According to popular notion, the genius learns without
    study, and knows without learning. He is eloquent without
    preparation, exact without calculations and profound without
    reflection.
                Barlow, 1951, 142.
    3. Is something inexplicable and unaccountable, some gift we
    possess apart from any merit or effort on our own, it is innate
    and not acquired.
                Barlow, 1951, 145..
    4. Like intelligence, is never seen directly; it is seen only
    in its results—superior performance of some kind.
                Gold, 1965, 6.
    5.(a) A person of exceptionally high mental ability, frequently
    evidenced by superior powers of invention or origination or by
    exceptional performance in some special skill, such as music,
    art, or mechanics;
    (b) Exceptional ability as defined above. (No specific level of
    ability has been universally accepted as indicative of genius,

although an I.Q. of 140 or more has sometimes been used as an arbitrary standard.)
Good, 1973, 259.
6. The term has been applied to outstanding individuals who have attained eminence in some field of intellectual or creative endeavor. Sometimes the individual is recognized as a child prodigy at a young age; sometimes he is not recognized as 'great' until he has become known for a unique contribution at a later stage of his life or in some instances after his death.
Kirk & Gallagher, 1979, 69
7. Those men who are able to arouse permanently, and in the highest degree, that positive, scientifically grounded feeling of worth and value in a wide group of human beings.
Kretschmer, 1931, 9.
8. In the sense that they (gifted children) become known for their outstanding contributions (or damages) to mankind in some notable field of achievement.
Laycock, 1967, 9.

GEOGRAPHIC ISOLATION
The condition of being geographically located away from the mainstream of society.
Baldwin, 1978, 1.

GIFT
Any ability possessed by a person to a high degree, frequently manifested by achievement without apparent effort.
Good, 1973, 261.

GIFTED
1. Used in reference to extremely gifted, moderately gifted and talented (children).
Brain, 1960, 3.
2. Refers to people who have developed high levels of intellectual ability or who show promise of such development.
Clark, 1979, 5.
3. Students with superior cognitive abilities include approximately the top 3 percent of the general school population in measured general intelligence and/or in creative abilities or other talents that promise to make lasting contributions of merit to society. These students are so able that they require special provisions if appropriate educational opportunities are to be provided for them.
Dunn, 1973, 193.
4. Applies to those students who have a very high level of academic aptitude, either demonstrated or potential. ...Terms

that will be used interchangeably with gifted include "bright,"
"superior," "fast learning," and "academically talented."

Durr, 1964, 16.

5. Encompasses those children who possess a superior
intellectual potential and functional ability to achieve
academically in the top 15 to 20 percent of the school
population; and 1 or more talent of a high order in such special
areas as mathematics, mechanics, science, expressive arts,
creative writing, music, and social leadership; and a unique
creative ability to deal with their environment.

Fliegler and Bish, 1959, 409.

6. Refer to those with intellectual or academic capabilities
that exceed a majority of their age mates.

French, 1959, 4.

7. (A child) who is superior in some ability that can make him
an outstanding contributor to the welfare of, and quality of
living in, society.

Havighurst, 1961, 528.

8. A person whose development and behavior—apart from sheer
physical superiority—consistently demonstrates unusual traits,
capacities, and achievements for his age.

Hildreth, 1966, 23.

9. (Refers to a child) who is significantly superior in terms
of intellectual ability. The actual I.Q. score and criteria
for determining giftedness vary from state to state and from
area to area.

L'Abate and Curtis, 1975, 5.

10. (A term) referring to a high degree of general intellectual
ability or of high general intelligence.

Laycock, 1967, 9.

11. A group so advanced that they require special attention
beyond the usual school provisions.

Martinson, 1977, 5.

12. a) Given the total continuum of general "intelligence" the
gifted are perceived as falling along the higher range.
b) Those children whose anticipated superior social contribution
is primarily a function of their superior conceptualization
capacity.

Newland, 1976, 24.

13. Any child with an I.Q. of 120 or over whose performance is
constantly outstanding and having a potential value to the
welfare of society.

Otto, 1955, 3.

14. (A child) who has the capacity for superior achievement in
some area of human endeavor which has consistently made an
outstanding contribution to civilization. Such a broad

definition would include academic fields such as music, graphic and plastic art, performing and mechanical arts, and the field of human relations.
Passow, 1963, 3.
15. Those whose performance is consistently remarkable in any potentially valuable area.
Witty, 1940, 516.
16. Those who possess a superior nervous system characterized by the potential to perform tasks requiring a comparatively high degree of intellectual abstraction or creative imagination.
Sumption & Leucking, 1960, 6.
17. Refers to children who achieved 132 or higher on the Stanford Binet Intelligence Tests. These comprise the top 2 percent of the general population.
Syphers, 1972, 5.

GIFTED AND TALENTED CHILDREN
Children identified by professionally qualified persons who by virtue of outstanding abilities, are capable of high performance. These are children who require differentiated educational programs and/or services beyond those normally provided by the regular school program in order to realize their contribution to self and society.
Children capable of high performance include those with demonstrated achievement and/or potential ability in any of the following areas, singly or in combination (1) general intellectual ability, (2) specific academic aptitude, (3) creative or productive thinking, (4) leadership ability, (5) visual and performing arts, and (6) psychomotor ability.
Marland, 1972, 10.

GIFTED, EXTREMELY
A small fraction of the gifted group who have an exceedingly high level of ability and whose potential powers should enable them to make original and significant contributions to the welfare of their own and succeeding generations.
Good, 1973, 261.

GIFTED, MENTALLY
As applied to a child or youth possessing high intellectual ability, with mental age well in advance of the norm, and consequently a high IQ.
As applied to an adult possessing intellectual ability well above the average.
Good, 1973, 261.

GIFTEDNESS
1. A superior general intellectual potential and ability (approximate IQ 120+); a high functional ability to achieve in various academic areas commensurate with general intellectual ability; a high-order talent in such special areas as art, music, mechanical ability; foreign languages, science, mathematics, dramatics, social leadership, and creative writing and a creative ability to develop a novel event in the environment. This definition probably includes about 15 to 20 percent of the school populations.
Fliegler, 1961, 16.
2. An interaction among three basic clusters of human traits, these clusters being above average general abilities, high levels of task commitment, and high levels of creativity. Gifted and talented children are those possessing or capable at developing this composite set of traits and applying them to any potentially valuable area of human performance. Children who manifest or are capable of developing the interaction among the three clusters require a wide variety of educational opportunities and services that are not ordinarily provided through regular instructional programs.
Renzulli, 1978, 261.
3. A complex, multifaceted quality of human functioning that takes many different forms depending on the circumstances in which an individual grows up and the multiplicity of tasks and rewards that exist for him in a rapidly changing and imperfectly predictable world.
Thompson, 1972, 39.

GIFTED PROGRAMS, ARTICULATION: (See Articulation of Gifted Programs)

GIFTED STUDENT
A student possessing high skill or intellectual ability.
Hopke, 1968, 157.

GIFTED UNDERACHIEVER
A child with high intellectual ability who does not achieve on a level commensurate with his ability.
Good, 1973, 261.

GLOBAL I.Q.
A single score which represents the overall intellectual ability of the individual.
Good, 1973, 262.

GRADE SKIPPING
A provision that permits the accelerant to bypass the immediate higher grade level. It has been most commonly used in the elementary school.
Fliegler, 1961, 27.

GROUPING
1. Provisions that facilitate the students access to special learning opportunities. Cluster grouping within the regular class. Special regular classes, part-time groups before, during, after school or on Saturdays, seminars, minicourses, team teaching.
Correll, 1978, 25.
2. Refers to the administrative arrangement of organizing students into instructional units for purposes of accelerating and enriching the learning experiences of the gifted students. Grouping by chronological age is accepted administrative practice in all schools. Grouping by interest also meets little resistance. Grouping on the basis of intellectual ability or other talent, however, meets much greater resistance.
DeHaan & Havighurst, 1961, 91.

GROUPING, ABILITY: (See Ability Grouping)

GROUP INTELLIGENCE TESTS
A measurement device ordinarily used with more than one person at a time. More widely used than individual intelligence tests because of economy and efficiency of testing.
Owen, Blount and Moscow, 1978, 551.

GROUP TEST
A test designed to be administered to more than one person at a time.
Sax, 1980, 623.

GUIDED DISCOVERY: (See Discovery Learning)

H

HANDICAPPED, ACADEMICALLY

Students whose school achievement failed to live up to their expectancy level to such a degree that physicians, psychologists and/or educators feel that they would benefit from special considerations, special services or a special curriculum in their daily school routine; also called educationally retarded.

Good, 1973, 275.

HANDICAPPED GIFTED

A person of high intellectual or creative capacity who is...hard of hearing, deaf, speech impaired, visually handicapped, seriously emotionally disturbed, orthopedically impaired or other health impaired ...or with specific learning disabilities who by reason thereof require special education and related services.

Maker, 1977, 55.

HEMISPHERICITY

The tendency for a person to rely more on one than the other cerebral hemisphere in processing information. The left cerebral hemisphere seems to be specialized for the logical, sequential processing of information and deals primarily with verbal, analytical, abstract, temporal, and digital materials. The right cerebral hemisphere processes information nonlinearly, holistically, simultaneously dealing with a variety of variables and primarily non-verbal, concrete, spatial, analogic, emotional, and aesthetic materials.

Torrance and Mourad, 1979, 44.

HEMISPHERIC SPECIALIZATION

The adaptation of each half of the brain to particular, specialized functions. In humans, the left hemisphere specializes in cognitive, abstract reasoning, while the right hemisphere organizes perceptual and spatial stimuli. See also split brain.

Owen, Blount & Moscow, 1978, 551.

HENMON-NELSON TESTS OF MENTAL ABILITY, THE: (See Appendix D)

HEREDITARY GENIUS

An ability that was exceptionally high and at the same time unborn.

Galton, 1960, 9.

HIGHLY GIFTED
1. The child's intelligence is so exceptional that it is almost impossible for either home or school to satisfy his needs unless they too are equally exceptional. ...two main types—the 'moderately gifted' with I.Q.'s below 150 ...and the 'highly gifted' with I.Q.'s above that level. A child of this latter type may be as much ahead of the gifted children as these are ahead of the average child.
Burt, 1975, 170.
2. Those who are in the top percent of the total population with respect to intellectual capacity (that is, roughly, individuals with an IQ of 137).
EPC, 1950, 43.
3. At a given age level one child in 1,000 would, on the average, have a Binet IQ of 148 or above and such children comprise the highly gifted group.
Syphers, 1972, 5.

HOMOGENEOUS CLASS: (See Class, Homogeneous Special).

HONORS CLASS
A group selected for advanced instruction because of demonstrated high achievement; usually applied in secondary schools or colleges.
Good, 1973, 101.

HONORS COURSE
1. A course, at high school or college level, that limits enrollment to exceptionally capable students; provides for independent or tutorial work; places greater responsibility for student progress on the student; emphasizes reading and self instruction, and sometimes frees the student from regular classroom attendance and regular course requirements.
Hopke, 1968, 181.
2. A course, at high school or college level, that limits enrollment to exceptionally capable students; provides for independent or tutorial work, places the responsibility for student progress more on the student than on the teacher, emphasizes reading and self-instruction, and usually frees the student from regular classroom attendance and regular course requirements.
Good, 1973, 149.

HONORS PROGRAM
A program for superior students involving enrichment of the curriculum and opportunities for accelerating. The honors

program may extend through the entire curriculum or be available only to members of a certain class or be offered in single courses.

Hopke, 1968, 181.

HORIZONTAL ENRICHMENT: (See Enrichment Model, The).

HORIZONTAL GROUPING
Grouping by chronological age.
Bridges, 1973, 101.

I

IDEATIONAL FLUENCY

1. The ability to produce ideas to fulfill certain requirements in limited time... There are certain stages in most problem-solving where there must be a searching for answers... The scanning process is more likely to arrive at suitable solutions if it can elicit a greater number of possibilities. Thus ideational fluency probably plays an important role in problem-solving... Individuals who are high on scores for ideational fluency are inclined to be more impulsive, more ascendant, and more confident and to have a stronger appreciation of creativity.

Anderson, 1959, 146.

2. The ability to produce a variety of ideas of hypothesis concerning possible solutions to problems.

Torrance, 1963, 95.

IDENTIFICATION

1. The process of screening children by means of standardized test procedures and/or observational methods and selecting the superior children for educational programs designed particularly for them. A good identification program should discover other characteristics of gifted children besides their aptitudes and capacities.

DeHaan, 1957, 41-48.

2. A process which attempts to screen and select bright individuals in order to plan a program for them. The function of identification is to discover gifted children who evince superior ability.

Fliegler, 1961, 18.

3. Includes all of the information which can be gathered about a given pupil.

Martinson, 1977, 16.

4. The process of finding those students who meet the criteria of giftedness adopted in a given school or system.

SREB, 1962, 30.

I.E.P.: (See Individualized Education Program)

ILLUMINATION

The (third) stage (of four stages in the Creative Process) during which the "happy idea" occurs. It has been referred to as the "Aha Phenomenon." In this stage, the creator suddenly sees the idea, concept or solution to the problem.

Gallagher, 1975, 250.

IMPLICATIONS
Extrapolations of information, in the form of expectancies, predictions, known or suspected antecedents, concomitants, or consequences. The connection between the given information and that extrapolated is more general and less definable than a relational connection.
Meeker, 1969, 196.

INCUBATION
In this stage (the second of four stages in the Creative Process) the person is not consciously thinking about the problem. There is some kind of internal mental process which associates new information with past information. Some type of reorganization of the information seems to be going on without the individual being directly aware of it.
Gallagher, 1975, 249.

INDEPENDENT STUDY
A program of study with topics of problems chosen by the student with the approval of the department concerned and with the supervision of an instructor.
Hopke, 1968, 185.

INDEPENDENT STUDY: (See Self-Directed Study)

INDIRECT TEACHING
A style of instruction sometimes characterized as "student-centered," that is, it encourages students to share in classroom dialogue.
Owen, Blount and Moscow, 1978, 552.

INDIVIDUAL INTELLIGENCE TEST
A measurement device used with only a single person at a time. Believed to be somewhat more valid and reliable than group intelligence tests. A specialist is required to administer and interpret the individual test and this increases its cost.
Owen, Blount & Moscow, 1978, 552.

INDIVIDUALIZATION
A way of organizing learning experiences so that the rate content, schedule, experience, and depth of exploration available to all students stem from their assessed achievement and interests.
Clark, 1979, 182.

INDIVIDUALIZED CLASSROOMS
Provisions which make use of individual, team, flexible small group instruction. Assessments are used to determine the curriculum and materials for each student. The classroom is decentralized and gives access to many types of learning. In most cases such classes are ungraded with students from several age levels.
Clark, 1979, 141.

INDIVIDUALIZED EDUCATION PROGRAM (I.E.P.)
A provision of the Education for All Handicapped Children Act that requires schools to create a statement of specific plans for each handicapped student, to be developed with parents' assistance.
Owen, Blount, and Moscow, 1978, 552.

INDIVIDUAL TEST
A test designed to be administered to one person at a time. Such a test is usually given to observe how the individual responds.
Sax, 1980, 624.

INNER-DIRECTED PERSON
This type person adopted early in life a small number of values and principles which he rigidly adheres to no matter what the situation in which he finds himself is like.
Johnson, 1972, 3.

INNOVATIVE CREATIVITY
Creativity involving significant alterations in the basic foundations of the principles of a theory or situation in which the individual needs to possess and apply highly developed abstract skills of conceptualization.
Taylor, 1960, 6.

INQUIRY MODEL
A model in which the rationale is to aid students to become independent in their thinking. It requires the development of many skills (i.e. making careful observations, asking good questions, comparing, discovering relevant data, summarizing, and generalizing from data).
Clark, 1979, 203.

INQUIRY TEACHING
A systematic way of planning problem-solving tasks and posing questions which will promote "independent" (guided)

solution-finding activities by students. Its main objective is to train students' problem-solving skills.
Kuo, 1976, 137.

INQUIRY TRAINING

A program to supplement the ordinary science classroom activities. It gives the child a plan of operation that will help him to discover causal factors of physical change through his own initiative and control, and not to depend on the explanations and interpretations of teachers or other knowledgeable adults. He learns to formulate hypotheses, to test them through verbal form of controlled experimentation, and to interpret the results. In a nutshell, the program is aimed at making pupils more independent, systematic, empirical, and inductive in their approach to problems of science.
Suchman, 1960, 42.

INSTRUCTIONAL ACCELERATION

Those practices of teachers which enable pupils to undertake learning activities usually engaged in by pupils who are older than they are. Two forms are: (a) Horizontal—something added at the present level, and (b) Vertical—something added above the present level.
Newland, 1976, 249.

INTELLECTUAL GIFTEDNESS

Abilities and capacities, but more often in normative or statistical fashion. Children are considered gifted if they surpass a given I.Q. score or fall within a designated percentage of a total population. These persons are called gifted, bright, academically able or intellectually superior. Other terms imply both capacity and achievement. These terms include learner, or academically able and ambitious student.
Freehill, 1962, 8.

INTELLIGENCE

1. A composite or combination of human traits which includes a capacity for insight into complex relationships, all of the processes involved in abstract thinking, "adaptability in problem solving, and capacity to acquire new capacity."
Cattell, 1971, 8.
2. The capacity to learn; the sum total of knowledge acquired by an individual; the ability to adjust or to adapt to the total environment.
Suran & Rizzo, 1979, 490.
3. The entire repertoire of acquired skills, knowledge,

learning sets, and generalization tendencies considered intellectual in nature that are available at any one period in time.
Cleary, Humphreys, Kendrick, 1975, 19.
4. The aggregate or global capacity to act purposefully, to think rationally, and to deal effectively with the environment.
Wechsler, 1958, 7.

INTELLIGENCE TEST
An instrument used for measuring intellectual functioning, the ability to learn or the ability to deal with new situations.
Good, 1973, 598.

INTEREST
1. A form of selective awareness of attention that produces meaning out of the mass of one's experiences.
Skinner, 1959, 337.
2. A tendency to prefer or engage in a particular type of activity. Interest tests tend to focus on occupational and educational interests, and to assess them through the individual's selection of activities that he would like to engage in.
Thorndike, 1969, 649.
3. Interest denotes a more extensive reaction to a condition or phenomenon. It is more than incipient reaction; in fact, to be "interested" in something, one usually has to have had some modicum of successful relationship with it. More generally, interest is an approach behavior tendency which results from a psychological sum of successful experiences in some area of activity, multiplied by the individual's capability of understanding, or comprehending, the components to which he is reacting (and the relationships among them), divided by the psychological sum of his unsuccessful experiences in such involvement.
Newland, 1976, 41.

INTERPERSONAL EFFECTIVENESS
The degree of which the consequences of your behavior match your intentions.
Johnson, 1972, 18.

INTRA-CLASSROOM PROTOTYPES
Prototypes which are placed within the context of the regular classroom program.
Kaplan, 1977, 46.

INVENTIVE CREATIVITY
Creativity involving ingenuity in visualizing new uses for old parts where no new basic idea is involved.
Taylor, 1960, 6.

IQ, DEVIATION: (See Deviation IQ)

K

KINESTHETICALLY GIFTED, THE
   A high level of visual, performing arts, or psychomotor skills
often is referred to as kinesthetic giftedness.
            Walker, 1978, 477.

L

LATENT ACHIEVER

A person who possesses hidden ability to succeed in specified areas but who has not yet reached the culmination stage of this process, possibly because of developmental or motivational factors. (See Underachievement).

Good, 1973, 7.

LEADERSHIP

1. a) The ability and readiness to inspire, guide, direct, or manage others; b) the role of interpreter of the interests and objectives of a group; the group recognizing and accepting the interpreter as spokesman.

Good, 1973, 332.

2. The process of influencing others in making decisions, setting goals and achieving goals...and, concurrently, it is the process of keeping the group voluntarily together.

Lawson, Griffin, & Donant, 1977, 176.

LEARNING

1. A hypothetical process within the organism, inferred by observing lasting changes in performance.

Owen, Blount, and Moscow, 1978, 553.

2. A modification of behavior as a result of experience or training.

Perkins, 1974, 455.

LEARNING DISORDERS

(Usually abbreviated L.D.) A broad class of symptoms that show difficulty in mastering one or more school subjects. Commonly, a learning disordered youngster shows normal intelligence, but sub-average performance in certain tasks (often reading).

Owen, Blount, and Moscow, 1978, 553.

LORGE-THORNDIKE INTELLIGENCE TEST: (See Appendix D)

M

MAT: Metropolitan Achievement Test (See Appendix D)

MEMORY (SOI)
Retention or storage, with some degree of availability of information in the same form it was committed to storage and in response to the same cues in connection with which it was learned.
Meeker, 1969, 195.

MENTAL ABILITY
An inclusive term, more properly referred to as "capacity", and including such conceptions as intelligence and aptitude (talent) and related processes such as creativity, productive thinking, divergent thinking etc.
SREB, 1962, 30.

MENTAL AGE
The age level at which an individual performs on an intelligence test. For example, a mental age (MA) of 8-0 means that the individual obtained the same score as an average group of eight year olds.
Sax, 1980, 626.

MENTALLY ADVANCED
Above the average group in intelligence.
Good, 1973, 362.

MENTALLY SUPERIOR, EDUCATION OF THE
The provision of materials and methods of instruction suitable for pupils of high or superior intelligence, by means of such techniques as a) enrichment of course of study; b) acceleration, that is, rapid promotion; c) adaptation of subject matter through individual instruction; d) homogeneous grouping; and e) special classes for superior pupils.
Good, 1973, 362.

MENTAL TESTS
Devices such as intelligence, aptitude, achievement, and personality tests, or rating scales for various skills, which are designed to provide relatively objective means of assessing or comparing certain of the capacities of characteristics of individuals.
SREB, 1962, 30.

MENTOR PROGRAM
   (A program whereby) some students are so advanced they need the
   challenge of an outside expert.
         Clark, 1979, 215.

METROPOLITAN ACHIEVEMENT TEST: (See Appendix D)

MFS-A
   Memory for a figural system. The ability to remember auditory
   complexes of rhythm or melody.
         Meeker, 1969, 52.

MFS-V
   Memory for a figural system—visual. The ability to remember
   the spatial order or placement of given visual information.
         Meeker, 1969, 52.

MFU
   Memory for figural units. The ability to remember given figural
   objects.
         Meeker, 1969, 51.

MINORITIES
   A racial, religious, or political group that is part of, but
   differs from, a larger controlling group.
         Webster, 1968, 477.

MINORITY GROUP CHILD
   A child whose parents are classified according to race,
   religion, or nationality as belonging to groups whose membership
   is less than 50 percent of a given population.
         Good, 1973, 96.

MMC
   Memory for semantic classes. The ability to remember verbal or
   ideational class properties.
         Meeker, 1969, 58.

MMI
   Memory for semantic implications. The ability to remember
   arbitrary connections between pairs of meaningful elements of
   information.
         Meeker, 1969, 60.

MMR
   Memory for semantic relations. The ability to remember

meaningful connections between items of verbal information.
Meeker, 1969, 59.

MMS

Memory for a semantic system. The ability to remember
meaningful ordered verbal information.
Meeker, 1969, 59.

MMT

Memory for semantic transformations. The ability to remember
changes in meaning or redefinitions.
Meeker, 1969, 60.

MMU

Memory for a semantic unit. The ability to remember isolated
ideas or word meanings.
Meeker, 1969, 58.

MODERATELY GIFTED

(Applies) to individuals who fall within the top 10 percent but
below the top 1 percent (that is, between 120 and 137 I.Q.).
EPC, 1950, 43.

MODIFIED ABILITY GROUPING

The organizational pattern is established so that the superior
youngsters participate with their intellectual peers in academic
subjects for only part of the day and participate with their
chronological age peers in peripheral subject areas for the
remainder of the day. The time spent in the special may vary
with the situation, one-half of the day being considered
optimum.
Fliegler, 1961, 25.

MORPHOLOGICAL ANALYSIS

A technique that involves studying two or more components of a
problem. It focuses on a principle of combinations. In
morphological analysis an attempt is made to try to combine
existing data or parts of a problem in new ways, to discover
original ideas or solutions. It usually employs a grid or
matrix to help in the study of as many combinations as possible,
in a systematic manner.
Feldhusen & Treffinger, 1977, 42.

MOTIVATION

1.   Stimulation to make full use of abilities in any

direction.

Bridges, 1973, 27.

2. a) Includes the concept of need, affiliation, incentives, habit, discrepancy, and innate curiosity. b) A hypothetical construct to explain the initiation, direction, intensity, and persistence of goal-directed behavior.

Good and Brophy, 1977, 327-328.

3. a) The forces that promote action toward attaining goals and obtaining results. The practical art of applying incentives and arousing interest for the purpose of causing a pupil to perform in a desired way. b) A combination of forces that promotes positive action toward the attainment of realistic goals, resulting in feelings of self-worth.

Hopke, 1968, 228.

4. A hypothetical process that is inferred from goal-directed behavior. Motivation is not an observable process, and it cannot be measured directly.

Lazerson, 1975, 357.

5. Denotes relatively "self-sustained" application to a task to achieve some personally or socially acceptable outcome. It is an avid drive for knowledge because of satisfaction of learning and discovering. It denotes the operation of conditions, either outside or within the individual, which are conducive to his responding in certain ways, or which dispose him to react in certain ways. Usually, it is regarded as getting the individual to "want" to do something.

Newland, 1976, 105.

MSC

Memory for symbolic classes. The ability to remember symbolic class properties.

Meeker, 1969, 54.

MSI

Memory for symbolic implications. The ability to remember arbitrary connections between symbols.

Meeker, 1969, p. 57.

MSR

Memory for symbolic relations. The ability to remember definitive connections between units of symbolic information.

Meeker, 1969, 54.

MSS

Memory for symbolic system. The ability to remember the order

of symbolic information.
>Meeker, 1969, 56.

MST

Memory for symbolic transformations. The ability to remember changes in symbolic information.
>Meeker, 1969, 56.

MSU

Memory for symbolic units. The ability to remember isolated items of symbolic information, such as syllables and words.
>Meeker, 1969, 53.

MULTICULTURALITY

(A term) invented to express the concept of assimilating aspects of different cultures.
>Plowman, 1972, 130.

MULTIPLE TRACKING (see Tracking)

MULTIPOTENTIAL

Refers to any individual who, when provided with an appropriate environment, can select and develop any number of competencies to a high level. He is a person who seemingly is able to adapt his performances and is, therefore well suited for a world in which there is much change. For those who can adapt and still exhibit high levels of performance, there is a premium on their contributions to mankind and their own personal satisfactions.
>Fredrickson and Rothney, 1972, vii.

N

NAGC: (See National Association for Gifted Children, Appendix B)

NATURE VERSUS NURTURE CONTROVERSY
A controversy espoused by both those who contended that intelligence is inherited and fixed (nature) and those who believed that intelligence is changed if a child is placed in a favorable and stimulating environment (nurture).
Perkins, 1974, 502.

NFC
Convergent production of a figural classification. The ability to classify, uniquely or conventionally, items of figural information.
Meeker, 1969, 75.

NFT
Convergent production of figural transformations. The ability to break down given figural units to form new ones. Locating faces or objects hidden in complex pictorial scenes describes this ability.
Meeker, 1969, 76.

NMC
Convergent production of semantic classes. The ability to produce verbally meaningful classes under specific conditions and restrictions.
Meeker, 1969, 82.

NMI
Convergent production of semantic implications. The ability to deduce meaningful information implicit in the given information.
Meeker, 1969, 84.

NMR
Convergent production of semantic relations. The ability to produce a word or idea that conforms to specific relationship requirements.
Meeker, 1969, 83.

NMS
Convergent production of semantic systems. The ability to order information into a verbally meaningful sequence.
Meeker, 1969, 83.

NMT

Convergent production of a semantic transformation. The ability to produce new uses for objects by taking them out of their given context and redefining them.

Meeker, 1969, 84.

NMU

Convergent production of semantic units. The ability to converge on an appropriate name (or summarizing word) for any given information.

Meeker, 1969, 81.

NONGRADED SCHOOL

A school which groups its students according to academic ability, disciplinary problems, and mental and physical capabilities rather than strictly by grade and age, each student progressing at his or her own rate.

Good, 1973, 387.

NONVERBAL INTELLIGENCE TEST

1. A device used for measuring intelligence without the use of speech or language by examiner or subject; frequently tests requiring little speech or language are referred to as nonverbal; such tests indicate the ability to work efficiently to solve the problems that do not involve verbal symbols.

Good, 1973, 599.

2. A test that does not require the use of words in the item or in the response to it. (Oral directions may be included in the formulation of the task.) A test cannot, however, be classified as nonverbal simply because it does not require reading on the part of the examinee. The use of nonverbal tasks cannot completely eliminate the effect of culture.

Mehrens & Lehmann, 1978, 697.

NORM GROUP

Sometimes called a standardization group; it consists of those persons selected to be representative of specified populations, such as third graders in the United States or applicants for specified types of jobs.

Sax, 1980, 626.

NORM REFERENCED TESTS

Standardized or specifically constructed; intelligence or achievement; individual or group. Norm referenced measures use

the performance of other individuals as the standard by which the student is compared.
> Clark, 1979, 123.

NORMS
Summarized statistics that describe the test performance of reference groups of pupils of various ages or grades in the standardization group for the test. Grade, age, standard score, and percentile are common types of norms.
> Robb, Bernardoni, & Johnson, 1972, 338.

NSC
Convergent production of symbolic classes. The ability to classify uniquely items of symbolic information.
> Meeker, 1969, 78.

NSI
Convergent production of symbolic implications. The ability to produce a completely determined symbolic deduction from given symbolic information, where the implication has not been practiced as such.
> Meeker, 1969, 80.

N/S/L TI G/T: (see National/State Leadership Training Institute on the Gifted and Talented; Appendix B).

NSR
Convergent production of symbolic relations. The ability to complete a specified symbolic relationship.
> Meeker, 1969, 79.

NSS
Convergent production of a symbolic system. The ability to produce a fully determined order or sequence of symbols.
> Meeker, 1969, 79.

NST
Convergent production of symbolic transformations. The ability to produce new symbolic items of information by revising given items.
> Meeker, 1969, 80.

O

OGT: (See Office of the Gifted and Talented, Appendix B)

OPERATIONS (SOI)
Major or kinds of intellectual activities or processes; things that the organism does with the raw materials of information, information being defined as that which the organism discriminates.
Meeker, 1969, 195.

ORIGINALITY
1. The ability to make unusual responses, to organize things in uncommon ways, and to be novel at their present level of overall development. What might be called original in a child might not be original for an adult. What might be termed original within a given individual's experience might not be original for a larger group of people.
McFee, 1970, 163.
2. Refers to infrequent, unusual, or remote responses.
Walker, 1978, 476.
3. In the measurement of creativity, the infrequency or rarity of a response.
Owen, Blount, & Moscow, 1978, 556.
4. The ability to produce uncommon responses; remote, unusual, or unconventional associations; cleverness.
Torrance, 1963, 96.
5. The ability to produce ideas that not many people think of or that are unusual, remote and clever.
Khatena, 1978, 25.

OTHER-DIRECTED PERSON
A person that receives guidance and direction from the people he relates to; his behavior conforms rigidly to whatever is necessary to gain the approval of other people.
Johnson, 1972, 3.

OTIS-LENNON MENTAL ABILITY TEST: (See Appendix D)

OVERACHIEVEMENT
A level of accomplishment which extends above and beyond the level of expectation as indicated by a comprehensive assessment of an individual's potentiality.
Good, 1973, 405.

OVERACHIEVERS

1. Those people...accomplishing at a higher rate of performance than the average of the class. For the ability or potential which they have, they are accomplishing at a higher level than would be expected of them.

Hopke, 1968, 259.

2. A term generally taken to refer to those students who have achievement test scores that are higher than what would have been predicted by intelligence test scores. Rather than referring to students as being overachievers, it is more accurate to refer to achievement scores as being higher than predicted by intelligence test scores. The emphasis is removed from a characterization of the student to the failure of a test to predict accurately.

Sax, 1980, 627.

P

PACE: (See Pre Accelerated College Enrollment Program)

PARTIAL SEGREGATION
Segregation of the gifted for some of their academic work or in order to provide for special seminars or honor classes.
Laycock, 1967, 54.

PEABODY PICTURE VOCABULARY TEST: (see Appendix D)

PEER TUTORING
Also termed "peer teaching" and "cross-age tutoring," an instructional method that uses a peer as a major teaching resource.
Owen, Blount, & Moscow, 1978, 556.

PERCENTILE
One of the 99 point scores that divide a ranked distribution into groups, each of which contains 1/100 of the scores. A percentile rank is a person's rank in a standard group of 100 persons representative of the full range of the normative population. If a person obtains a percentile rank of 70, his standing is regarded as equaling or surpassing 70 percent of the normative group on which the test was standardized; a percentile rank score of 70 may also be interpreted to mean that 30 percent of the normative group excel this person's test performance.
Robb, Bernardoni & Johnson, 1972, 330.

PERSISTENCE
One of the predisposing factors described by Brandwein. It is characterized as consisting of three attitudes: (1) A marked willingness to spend time, beyond the ordinary schedule, in a given task...(2) A willingness to withstand discomfort...and (3) A willingness to face failure.
Brandwein, 1955, 10.

PERSON, AUTONOMOUS: (See Autonomous Person)

PERSON, INNER-DIRECTED: (See Inner-Directed Person)

PERSON, OTHER-DIRECTED: (See Other-Directed Person)

PLACEMENT, ADVANCED: (See Advanced Placement)

POWER AND SENSITIVITY OF THOUGHT
   Ready grasp of principles underlying things as they are;
   sensitivity to inference in fact, consequence of proposition,
   application of idea; spontaneous elevation of immediate
   observations to higher planes of abstraction, imagination,
   meaningful association of ideas, forceful reasoning, original
   interpretations and conclusions, discriminatory power, quick
   detection of similarities and differences among things and
   ideas; able in analysis, synthesis, and organization of
   elements; critical of situations, self, and other people.
          SREB, 1962, 28.

PPVT: Peabody Picture Vocabulary Test (See Appendix D)

PRE-ACCELERATED COLLEGE ENROLLMENT PROGRAM (PACE)
   Students from grades 8-10 can enroll in regular university
   courses for university credit to be banked as in the ACE
   program. Enrollment is limited to summer; not more than two
   courses can be taken in one summer.
          Clark, 1979, 216.

PRECOCIOUS CHILD
   A child who is exceptionally advanced beyond the norm mentally
   or physically.
          Good, 1973, 96.

PREDISPOSING FACTOR
   Factors described by Brandwein as characteristics of success in
   scientific research. See: Questing and Persistence.
          Brandwein, 1955, 9.

PREDISPOSITION
   An inherited capacity of an individual to develop a certain
   trait or attribute. (The capacity is transmissible genetically,
   but the attribute or trait does not necessarily appear unless
   the proper constitutional and environmental factors coexist.)
          Good, 1973, 433.

PREPARATION
   The first stage of four stages in the Creative Process in which
   the problem is investigated from all directions and is primarily
   a problem identification and fact-gathering period.
          Gallagher, 1975, 249.

PROBLEM SOLVING
   The process of recognizing an obstacle, difficulty, or inability

to act; thinking of possible solutions; and testing or evaluating the solutions.

Feldhusen & Treffinger, 1977, 33.

PROBLEM-SOLVING TECHNIQUES
The creative process by which individuals evaluate changes in themselves and their environment, and make new choices, decisions, or adjustments in harmony with, life goals which may also be in a state of flux.

Hopke, 1968, 279.

PROCESS APPROACH
Investigation of mental processes involved in creative problem solving.

Owen, Blount & Moscow, 1978, 557.

PRODIGY
A person excessively advanced beyond the norm usually applied to cases of exceptionally high intelligence or extreme talent of a particular sort, as in music or art.

Good, 1973, 440.

PRODUCT APPROACH
Assessing a person's creativity by judging his creative products, such as a work of art, a publication or an invention.

Owen, Blount & Moscow, 1978, 557.

PRODUCTIVE CREATIVITY
Creativity in which the individual produces intellectual products by way of mastery over some portion of the environment.

Taylor, 1960, 6.

PRODUCTS (SOI)
The organization that information takes in the organism's processing of it.

Meeker, 1969, 196.

PROGRAM, ACCELERATION: (See Acceleration Program)

PROGRAM, ADVANCED PLACEMENT: (See Advanced Placement Program)

PROGRAM, ENRICHMENT
Extension of the curriculum to provide additional educational opportunities for gifted and bright children.

Good, 1973, 444.

PROGRAMMED LEARNING

Offers student a way to move at their own pace through skill-level learning. It includes individual assessment and allows students continuous feedback on work that is done at their own level.

Clark, 1979, 183.

PROGRAM PROTOTYPES

Program prototypes are organizational patterns which become the setting for the learning environment that accommodates the needs of the gifted and talented. (See Intra-classroom prototypes and Extra-classroom prototypes).

Kaplan 1977, 37.

PROTAGONIST

The term for the person who is the subject of the psychodramatic enactment. (see Psychodrama).

Blatner, 1973, 6.

PSEUDO-GIFTED CHILD

A child who having displayed certain gifts at an early age has been coached and pushed beyond his mental ability with resulting emotional strain and inability to maintain early levels of achievement.

Good, 1973, 96.

PSYCHODRAMA

The method by which a person can be helped to explore the psychological dimensions of his problems through the enactment of his conflict situation, rather than by talking about them.

Blatner, 1973, 6.

PSYCHOMOTOR

Pertaining to muscular action which follows directly from a mental process important in vocabulary proficiency, the performing arts, and sports.

Good, 1973, 459.

PSYCHOSOCIAL GIFTEDNESS

Includes superiority in political and social leadership and consists of an ability to facilitate attainment of group goals and to improve interpersonal relations within the group.

Walker, 1978, 476.

PUBLIC LAW 94-142: (See Education for All Handicapped Children)

Q

QUESTING

A term used by Brandwein to describe a notable dissatisfaction with present explanations of the way the world works—in short, a dissatisfaction with present explanations of aspects of reality...The "so what" attitude is not characteristic of questing; the general acceptance of authority in a given field of scholarship without question and without ascertaining the reliability and validity of the authority is not characteristic of questing; the belief that all is well in this best of all possible worlds is not questing. Questing is not Panglossian. Questing arises in a dissatisfaction. Questing, indeed, results in curiosity, in asking "Why?" "How?" or in the three perennials as the writer sees them: What Do We Know?, How Do We Know What We Know? and How Well Do We Know What We Know?
Brandwein, 1955, 10-11.

QUOTIENT, DEVIATION INTELLIGENCE

A measure of intelligence based on the extent to which an individual's score deviates from a score that is normal for the individual's age; it is standard score, not a quotient, with an arbitrarily assigned mean, usually 100, and a standard deviation usually 15 or 16, for all age levels.
Good, 1973, 465.

QUOTIENT, GROUP INTELLIGENCE

An intelligence quotient obtained from a group intelligence test rather than from an individual intelligence test.
Good, 1973, 456.

R

RAPID PROGRESS
...Allows the individual to complete the regular academic program by compressing two years into one, or lengthening the school year, or taking extra courses during the academic year.
Fliegler, 1961, 27.

RATING SCALE
Any number of structured techniques used to record observations systematically.
Sax, 1980, 618.

RELATIONS (SOI)
Connections between items of information based on variables or parents of contact that apply to them. Relational connections are more meaningful and definable than implications.
Meeker, 1969, 196.

RELEVANT CURRICULUM
A set of experiences which deals with topics and issues that youngsters would talk about if given a free choice.
Renzulli, 1973, 437-444.

RESOURCE PERSON (TEACHER/CONSULTANT)
A specialist in education of the gifted would travel to heterogeneously mixed classrooms to consult with teachers, work with gifted children in the room, and do demonstration teaching in cooperation with the regular teacher. In addition the teacher/consultant would prepare resources and learning kits, would extend the regular curriculum and provide appropriate challenge. One advantage here is that the classroom teacher has a supplemental source of teaching strategies and differentiated materials and can gradually assume more independence and responsibility for the programming.
White, 1978, 57.

RESOURCE TEACHER
A teacher specializing in one subject field (such as music, science, or physical education) who teaches on an itinerant basis usually in elementary grades, to supplement instructional offerings of the regular classroom teachers in self-contained classroom situations.
Good, 1973, 486.

S

SCALE, INTELLIGENCE
An instrument used to provide a measure of intelligence, constructed in accordance with the scale principle; often having exercises of increasing difficulty corresponding to levels of mental ability; loosely, used as a synonym for intelligence test.
Good, 1973, 508.

SCHOLASTIC APTITUDE: (See Academic Aptitude)

SCHOOL FOR THE MENTALLY SUPERIOR
A type of school devoted entirely to the education of pupils of high intelligence, presumably permitting more complete and effective organization of methods and materials for this purpose, than is provided in an ordinary school.
Good, 1973, 513.

SCREENING
The act or process of administering a screen test and applying its results.
Good, 1973, 521.

SECOND-ORDER GIFTED
Refers to the remaining children in the upper 10 percent in a given ability.
Havighurst, 1961, 528.

SELECTIVE ACCELERATION
The child retains his "basic" educational placement for most of his academic work but is enabled to take certain subjects or courses with classes or groups at higher designated grade levels.
Newland, 1976, 251.

SELF-ACTUALIZATION
1. Consists primarily of being time-competent, that is, of having the ability to tie the past and the future to the present in meaningful continuity while fully living in the present. The self-actualized person appears to be less burdened by guilts, regrets, and resentments from the past than is the nonself-actualizing person, and his aspirations are tied meaningfully to present working goals.
Johnson, 1972, 2.
2. The self-actualizing person is a person who appears to be

using all of his talents and gifts...Examples of people who fit Maslow's criteria of self-actualization would be Abraham Lincoln, Thomas Jefferson, Albert Schweitzer, Eleanor Roosevelt, Pablo Casals, Pierre Renoir, and Benjamin Franklin.
Gallagher, 1975, 243.

SELF-CONCEPT
1. The effective variable that refers to the view one has of one's self. A person with a positive self-concept considers himself or herself worthwhile. A negative self-concept means the person feels worthless.
Owen, Blount & Moscow, 1978, 559.
2. Self-concept is composed of all the beliefs and attitudes people have about themselves. It actually determines who they are. It also determines what they think they are, what they do, and what they become.
Canfield & Wells, 1976, 1.
3. Comprised of highly differentiated perceptions, beliefs, feelings, attitudes, and values that the individual views as part or characteristic of himself. The self-concept is formed as one identifies those aspects, qualities, ideas, and things that he regards as "me" and "mine".
Perkins, 1974, 249.

SELF-DIRECTED LEARNING
Concerned with creating an environment in which the learner manages and directs his or her efforts towards the attainment of specific goals.
Treffinger, 1975, 48.

SELF-DIRECTED OR INDEPENDENT STUDY
Provisions for self-selection of learning activities and materials.
Clark, 1979, 183.

SELF-DISCLOSURE
Revealing how you are reacting to the present situation and giving any information about the past that is relevant to understanding how you are reacting to the present. Reactions to people and events are not facts as much as feelings. To be self-disclosing means to share with another person how you feel about something he has done or said, or how you feel about the events which have just taken place. Self-disclosure does not mean revealing intimate details of your past life. (See Feedback).
Johnson, 1972, 10.

SELF-ESTEEM
Refers to the evaluation which the individual makes and customarily maintains with regard to himself. It expresses an attitude of approval or disapproval and indicates the extent to which the individual believes himself to be capable, significant, successful, and worthy.
Perkins, 1974, 251.

SEMANTIC (SOI).
Information in the form of meanings to which words commonly become attached, hence, most notable in verbal communication but not identical with words. Meaningful pictures also often convey semantic information.
Meeker, 1969, 196.

SIMULATION GAME
An activity in which participants interact within an artificially produced environment which recreates some aspect of social reality.
Cline, 1979, 270.

SITUATIONAL TEST
A contrived but lifelike task designed to measure how individuals will behave in a given situation without realizing they are being tested.
Sax, 1980, 631.

SITUATIONAL UNDERACHIEVERS
Those who underachieve only on occasion, as when a particularly difficult home problem erupts or a clash occurs with one particular teacher...
Clark, 1979, 279.

SLOSSON INTELLIGENCE TEXT: (See Appendix D)

SMPY: (See Study of Mathematical Precocious Youth)

SOCIALLY GIFTED
Adolescent boys and girls possesed of an exceptional capacity for mature productive relationships with others—both peers and adults...The child who exhibits unusual understanding and leadership of his peers.
Jarecky, 1959, 415.

SOCIODRAMA

A form of psychodramatic enactment which aims at clarifying group themes rather than focusing on the individual's problems. Although a person may participate as a protagonist in a sociodrama, the focus of the group task is on the problems of the role he plays in the drama rather than on his personal life situation. Thus sociodrama could be termed group-centered.
Blatner, 1973, 9.

SOCIOECONOMIC DEPRIVATION

A condition of legal or de facto denial of social interaction combined with substandard housing and jobs.
Baldwin, 1978, 1.

SOI (See Structure of Intellect).

SPECIAL CLASS

A provision which has the advantage of the special class with some integrated classes without the involvement with other groups that may be talented in other areas. The special class is most appropriate for the highly gifted.
Good, 1979, 142.

SPECIAL CLASSES

This "school within a school" concept may provide resource classes for the gifted, enrollment in regular college program courses while attending high school, Saturday sessions, and special summer programs. In most instances, special classes include provision of instruction for gifted children by temporarily removing them from their regular classes for a given amount of time prescribed by a planned schedule.
Walker, 1978, 489-490.

SPECIAL EDUCATION

The education of pupils (for example, the deaf, the blind, and partially seeing, the mentally subnormal, the gifted) who deviate so far physically, mentally, emotionally or socially from the relatively homogeneous group of so-called normal pupils that the standard curriculum is not suitable for their educational needs and their variations presents unusual management problems to the school through its interference with the learning of others; carried on in special classes, through special curriculum and/or special schools.
Good, 1973, 547.

SPECIAL SETTINGS MODEL, THE
Special classes, individual tutoring or foreign schooling may be designed to educate the student uniquely. Radically new methods, contents, sequences of subjects or levels of learning may be introduced. Special settings may range from the starkly traditional (e.g. foreign school) to the wildly experimental (e.g. self-programming). This is the only model capable of accommodating totally different curriculum expressly designed for the gifted.

SPLIT-BRAIN
Refers to the two hemispheres of the brain, often used in reference to brain research, or to specialization of the two hemispheres.
Owen, Blount & Moscow, 1978, 560.

STANDARDIZATION SAMPLE
Refers to that part of the reference population which is selected for use in norming a test. This sample should be representative of the reference population in essential characteristics, such as geographical representation, age and grade.
Robb, Bernardoni, & Johnson, 1972, 342.

STANDARDIZED TESTS
1. A standardized test is one that has been carefully constructed by experts in light of acceptable objectives or purposes; procedures for administering, scoring, and interpreting scores are specified in detail so that no matter who gives the test or where it may be given, the results should be comparable; norms or averages for different age or grade levels have been pre-determined. Certain types of standardized tests may also be designed to measure the degree of success on specified tasks.
Noll, Scannell, & Craig, 1965, 5.
2. As opposed to a teacher-made test, a standardized test is designed to be administered and scored under uniform testing conditions. Norms are also usually provided.
Sax, 1980, 633.

STANFORD-BINET INTELLIGENCE SCALE (S.B.) - Third Revision: (See Appendix D)

STANINE
A standard score obtained by dividing the normal curve into nine segments for the purpose of expressing scores in a single-digit

whole number from one to nine. Stanines of 1 and 9 contain the lowest and highest scoring 4 percent of individuals, respectively; stanines of 2 and 8, the next lowest and highest 7 percent; stanines of 3 and 7, the next 12 percent; stanines of 4 and 6, the next 17 percent; and stanine of 5, the middle 20 percent. When scores are converted to stanines, the shape of the original distribution is changed into a normal curve.
Sax, 1980, 633.

STREAMING
General ability grouping for all pupils.
Laycock, 1967, 54.

STRUCTURE OF INTELLECT (SOI)
1.   The Structure of Intellect is a model of intellectual abilities.   It is a product of a factor-analytic research conducted by J.P. Guilford and his associates in the Psychological Laboratory at the University of Southern California.   The Structure of Intellect conceptualizes intellectual abilities in a three-dimensional model.   Every intellectual ability in the structure is thus characterized in terms of the type of operation which is employed, the content involved, and the sort of product which results. The complete scheme is represented by a three-dimensional classification array of 120 predicted cells or categories of intellectual abilities.
Meeker, 1969, 7-9.
2.   The structure of intellect is a three-dimensional cube consisting of intellectual operations, products, and content. This model assumes that there are a total of 120 possible cognitive abilities.
Gallagher, 1975, 234.

STUDY OF MATHEMATICAL PRECOCIOUS YOUTH (SMPY)
1. A program which identifies and provides opportunities for students highly gifted in mathematics to accelerate directly from seventh to eighth grade into university classes.
Clark, 1979, 216.
2. A project at the Johns Hopkins University funded by the Spencer Foundation of Chicago. Dr. Julian C. Stanley is Director of SMPY. Drs. Daniel P. Keating and Lynn H. Fox are Associate Directors.
Stanley, Keating & Fox, 1974, xv.

SUMMATIVE EVALUATION
A decision reached near the end of a project that determines

whether it has been successful or not; contrasted with formative evaluation.

Sax, 1980, 633.

SUPERIOR CHILD

A child who is considerably above the norm in regard to a number of traits and abilities; usually applied to those children who have outstanding intellectual ability; frequently also implies better than usual social and physical development; a broader term than gifted child.

Good, 1973, 96.

SUPERIOR ENDOWMENT

Used to convey the idea of superior endowment: gifted, talented, superior, rapid learner, able student, bright, exceptional, and even genius.

Laycock, 1967, 9.

SYMBOLIC (SOI)

Information on the form of denotative signs, having no significance in and of themselves, such as letters, numbers, musical notations, codes, and words, when meanings and forms are not considered.

Meeker, 1969, 195.

SYNECTICS

A creative thinking technique that utilizes analogies and metaphors to help the thinker analyze problems and form different viewpoints.

Feldhusen & Treffinger, 1977, 45.

SYSTEMS (SOI)

Organized or structured aggregates of items of information; complexes of interrelated or interacting parts.

Meeker, 1969, 196.

T

TAG: (See Association for the Gifted, The; Appendix B)

TALENT
Any capacity for successful activity in a particular direction with which the immediate self of the individual is endowed.
Austin, 1925, 15.

TALENTED
1. All pupils who show unusual ability along non-academic lines and are capable of profiting from advanced instruction of making a career in their special field. The common denominator is the capacity for superior achievement and superior service.
Cutts & Mosely, 1957, 3.
2. A term most commonly applied to exceptional performance in such non-academic areas as sports, dramatics, dancing, music, arts and crafts, mechanical skills, and social leadership. (This) refers to specific performance rather than to potential. Genuine talent is the result of native ability, early spontaneous interest, and good training.
Hildreth, 1966, 33, 34, 39.
3. Refer(s) to those who excel in one or more of a wide variety of special abilities.
Laycock, 1967, 9.
4. Refers to persons of superior skills who do not necessarily show high intelligence.
Owen, Blount & Moscow, 1978, 560.
5. The type of individuals who did outstanding things in society, such as creative writing, singing, painting, acting, and erecting social leadership. These appear gifted even though they might not have met Binet IQ criterion.
Newland, 1976, 9.
6. Those who have demonstrated superior skill and whose promise is not primarily based on a function of their superior conceptualization capacity.
Newland, 1976, 24.

TALENT SECTIONING
The technique simply groups talented children together according to a subject area. Talent sectioning may be assessed in two ways: as an appendage to a regular course sequence; and as an integral part of a total program.
Fliegler, 1961, 24.

TAXONOMY OF EDUCATIONAL OBJECTIVES
A hierarchical classification scheme of the kinds of behavior we want students to acquire in educational settings. The three domains of the taxonomy of educational objectives are the cognitive domain, the affective domain, and the psychomotor domain. (See Affective Domain; Cognitive Domain and Psychomotor Domain).
Galloway, 1976, 47.

TEACHING STRATEGY
A method of organizing and presenting instructional materials and directing students' ways of dealing with the materials in order to elicit student's intellectual activitites.
Kuo, 1976, 7.

TEST
In the narrowest sense connotes the presentation of a standard set of questions to be answered.
Mehrens & Lehmann, 1978, 5.

TEST, ABILITY: (See Ability Test)

TEST, ACHIEVEMENT: (See Achievement Test)

TEST, CREATIVITY: (See Creativity Test)

TEST, CRITERION-REFERENCED: (See Criterion-Referenced Test)

TEST, CULTURE-FAIR: (See Culture-Fair Test)

TEST, DIAGNOSTIC: (see Diagnostic Test)

TEST, GROUP: (See Group Test)

TEST, INDIVIDUAL: (See Individual Test)

TEST, INTELLIGENCE: (See Intelligence Test)

TEST, NONVERBAL INTELLIGENCE: (See Nonverbal Intelligence Test)

TESTS, NORM REFERENCED: (See Norm Referenced Tests)

TEST, SITUATIONAL: (See Situational Test)

THINKING
   Results when there is persistent effort to examine the evidence
   which supports any belief, solution, or conclusion which is
   suggested for acceptance, together with the implications and
   further conclusions of the evidence.
                     Burton, 1960, v.

TORRANCE TESTS OF CREATIVE THINKING: (See Appendix D)

TOTAL ABILITY GROUPING
   A procedure to keep gifted children of similar ability together
   for the entire school day, whether it is practiced as the track
   plan in a comprehensive school or in a selective special school.

                     Fliegler, 1961, 22.

TOTAL INDIVIDUALIZATION
   Allows teacher and student to cooperatively assess and select
   goals, learning materials, activities, and instructional
   techniques.
                     Clark, 1979, 183.

TRACKING
   Tracking (or multiple tracking)—a form of educational
   organization in which pupils, usually of the same grade level,
   are assigned to three or more ability sections—fast, average,
   and slow learning, or further fractionations of these—with a
   view to facilitate their learning.
                     Newland, 1976, 262.

TRANSFORMATIONS (SOI)
   Changes of various kinds (redefinition, shifts, or modification)
   of ensuing information or of its function.
                     Meeker, 1969, 196.

TTCT: (See Torrance Tests of Creative Thinking, Appendix D)

TYPE I ENRICHMENT
   General exploratory activities. Consists of those experiences
   and activitites that are designed to bring the learner into
   touch with the kinds of topics or areas of study in which he or
   she may have a sincere interest. A good Type I Enrichment
   situation should involve very little structure, but at the same
   time, students and teachers should be aware that these
   situations have very purposeful objectives. By providing
   students with a wide variety of opportunities to become exposed

to different areas of potential interest, youngsters can begin to make their own decisions about the topics that they might like to explore at greater depths and higher levels of involvement.

Renzulli, 1977, 17.

TYPE II ENRICHMENT

Group training activitites. Consists of methods, materials, and instructional techniques that are mainly concerned with the development of thinking and feeling processes. The objective of Type II Enrichment is to develop in the learner the processes or operations (the "powers of mind") that enable him or her to deal more effectively with content.

Renzulli, 1977, 25.

TYPE III ENRICHMENT

Individual and small group investigation of real problems. Consists of activities in which the youngster becomes an actual investigator of a real problem or topic by using appropriate methods of inquiry.

Renzulli, 1977, 29.

U

UNDERACHIEVEMENT

1. Academic achievment at a level below the one expected on the basis of the student's performance on general aptitude tests and in the classroom. See latent achiever.

Good, 1973, 638.

2. Achievement which is below the level expected.

Sumption & Leucking, 1960, 145.

3. Failure to go as far in education as one's abilities would justify.

Havighurst, 1961, 528.

4. The broadest definition of underachievement among the more able would refer to all those who, for whatever reasons, fail to develop their potentialities maximally. A somewhat narrower definition of underachievement refers to all those individuals who demonstrate well above average intellectual or academic ability on intelligence and aptitude tests but fail to develop their abilities.

Raph, Passow, & Goldberg, 1966, 2-3.

UNDERACHIEVER

1. a. A person who falls below his capacity in school achievement. b. Those students particularly in high school, who fail in their studies or achieve results below standard for ability.

The bright student who used to be called a loafer is now known as an underachiever. The term applies to students whose school achievement does not come up to their high potential, the ones who receive low or mediocre grades in spite of high IQs. In some schools, he is the one who stands in the upper third or quarter of his class in ability as measured by objective tests, but falls in in the middle or lower segment in achievement, either in a particular subject or in his school work as a whole. The term has been applied to the bright or talented although slow learners who work below ability can also be called underachievers.

Hildreth, 1966, 422.

2. That portion of gifted youngsters who do not fulfill predicted academic performances from measures of cognitive ability.

Gallagher, 1975, 341.

3. A person with superior ability whose performance as judged by grades or achievement test scores, is significantly below his measured or demonstrated aptitudes or potential for academic achievment.

French, 1959, 320.

4. When educators talk of the underachiever, they are usually, (though not always) describing students who rank in the top third in intellectual ability, and whose performance is dramatically below that level.
Fine, 1967, 10.

5. The student who achieves below his potential. When examining this area, potential is generally defined in terms of intelligence, and achievement by teacher grades or standardized tests.
Durr, 1964, 41.

6. As contrasted with overachiever, the underachiever is an individual who has achievement test scores that are lower than those predicted by an intelligence test.
Sax, 1980, 634.

UNDERACHIEVER, CHRONIC: (See chronic underachiever)

UNDERACHIEVERS, SITUATIONAL: (See situational underachievers)

UNDERACHIEVING GIFTED STUDENT:
...Someone who has shown exceptional performance on a measure of intelligence and who, nevertheless, does not perform as well as expected for students of the same age on school related tasks.
Clark, 1979, 279.

UNDERACHIEVEMENT, DEFINED BY DURATION
Underachievement has always been classified or described according to its duration:
(a) Temporary/situational—the underachieving behavior has been precipitated by a temporary period of disturbance, such as divorcing parents, ill health, or a consuming new interest, or by a situation such as moving to a new school or experiencing a personality conflict with the teacher.
(b) Chronic—the pattern of underachieving behavior has been established for a long period of time and there are no indications that it is being created by a temporary situation.
Whitmore, 1980, 169-170.

UNDERACHIEVEMENT, DEFINED BY EFFECTS ON SELF AND OTHERS
The fourth criterion by which underachievement can be described is the effects of the underachievement on the individual and others:
(a) Mild to moderate—there are no evident negative effects on the underachiever or others in his life. His emotional adjustment and social behavior appear normal; the student does

not seem discontent or disturbed.

(b) Moderate to severe—the lack of success has created low self-esteem and self-derogatory attitudes, which have resulted in compensatory or coping behavior that impedes the individual's growth and may be socially destructive for the child. Two types of behavior patterns are typical: withdrawal and aggression. These coping mechanisms usually result in social isolation or peer alienation and continuous social conflict. Others in the underachiever's classroom may be negatively affected by his social behavior, and his family also is usually affected negatively as conflict increases at home.

Whitmore, 1980, 170.

UNDERACHIEVEMENT, DEFINED BY SCOPE

Underachievement can also be defined in terms of its scope:

(a) One specific ability—the student has the potential of achieving very well in a subject like math or art, or in a skill like handwriting or playing sports, but does not achieve particularly well because of a lack of interest or motivation. This type of underachievement is not regarded seriously by educators and may not warrant special educational programming for the child.

(b) One broad content area—usually the language-related subjects of reading, spelling, and language arts. Since this interrelated content area is basic to the entire instructional program, achievement in those subjects is considered very critical to overall academic success.

(c) General underachievement—the student is performing less well than his assessed aptitude would predict in all academic areas. There is no subject of the curriculum in which the student performs better than the average and he usually is below average.

Whitmore, 1980, 170.

UNDERACHIEVEMENT, KINDS OF

There are three kinds of underachievement defined by how the discrepancy between aptitude and achievement was revealed:

(a) Unknown—performance on aptitude and achievement measures are consistently low, hiding the ability of the child who is functionally untestable; or the student's underachievement is hidden by "satisfactory" performance and the teachers have no evidence that the student is capable of much higher achievement.

(b) High aptitude scores but low grades and achievement test scores.

(c) High standardized achievement test scores but low grades due to poor daily work, whether or not there are aptitude scores

that indicate the student's ability.
Whitmore, 1980, 169.

UNGUIDED DISCOVERY: (See Discovery Learning)

UNITS (SOI)
Relatively segregated or circumscribed items of information having "thing" character. May be close to Gestalt Psychology's "figure on a ground."
Meeker, 1969, 196.

UPWARD BOUND
A program designed to generate skills and motivation necessary for success in education beyond high school among young people from low-income backgrounds and to give them adequate secondary-school preparation, a cooperative program involving institutions of higher education and secondary schools; usually coordinated with activities of the Community Action Agencies and The Higher Education Act of 1965.
Good, 1973, 634.

VALUES

A preference for something cherished or desired; it is linked to one's satisfaction of needs, his realization of goals, and the maintenance and enhancement of his self-concept.
Perkins, 1974, 580.

VALUES CLARIFICATION

A series of activities meant to help students clarify their own feelings, attitudes, and values.
Owen, Blount & Moscow, 1978, 561.

VERIFICATION

The (fourth) stage (of four stages in the Creative Process) during which the idea which has been obtained through the first three stages is put to the test to see if it has validity or not.
Gallagher, 1975, 250.

VERTICAL ENRICHMENT: (See Enrichment Model, The)

VERTICAL GROUPING

Grouping based on factors rather than age.
Bridges, 1973, 102.

W

WECHSLER INTELLIGENCE SCALE FOR CHILDREN Revised (WISC-R: (see Appendix D))

Appendix A

BIBLIOGRAPHY

Adler, Sol
THE HEALTH AND EDUCATION OF THE ECONOMICALLY
DEPRIVED CHILD
St. Louis: Warren H. Green, Inc., 1968.

Albert, Robert S.
Toward a behavioral definition of genius.
THE INTELLECTUALLY GIFTED, Dennis W. & M.W.
Dennis (eds.)
New York: Grune & Stratton, 1976.

Anderson, Harold
CREATIVITY AND ITS CULTIVATION
New York: Harper & Row, 1969.

Austin, Mary
EVERYMAN'S GENIUS
Indianapolis: The Bobbs-Merrill Company Publishers, 1925.

Baldwin, Alexinia Y.
Introduction, EDUCATIONAL PLANNING FOR THE GIFTED:
OVERCOMING CULTURAL, GEOGRAPHIC, AND SOCIO-
ECONOMIC BARRIERS
Reston, Virginia: The Council for Exceptional Children, 1978.

Baldwin, A. & J. Wooster
BALDWIN IDENTIFICATION MATRIX INSERVICE KIT FOR
THE IDENTIFICATION OF GIFTED AND TALENTED
STUDENTS
Buffalo, New York: D.O.K., 1977.

Barlow, Fred
MENTAL PRODIGIES
New York: Hutchinson's Scientific and Technical Publications,
1951.

Bibliography 96

Bernal, Ernest M., Jr.
Gifted programs for the culturally different.
NASSP BULLETIN, 60-398
March 1976, 67-76.

Blanter, H.A.
ACTING-IN: PRACTICAL APPLICATIONS OF
PSYCHODRAMATIC METHODS
New York: Springer Publishing Company, 1973.

Bogen, J.E.
The other side of the brain: Parts I, II, and III. BULLETIN
OF THE LOS ANGELES NEUROLOGICAL SOCIETY
1969, 34, 73-105, 135-162, 191-203.

Brain, Russell
SOME REFLECTIONS ON GENIUS AND OTHER ESSAYS
Philadelphia: J.B. Lippincott Company, 1960.

Brandwein, P.F.
THE GIFTED STUDENT AS FUTURE SCIENTIST
New York: Harcourt, Brace, & Company, 1955.

Bridges, Sydney
I.Q.-150
London: Priory Press Limited, 1973.

Bruch, Catherine B.
Assessment of creativity in culturally different children.
THE GIFTED CHILD QUARTERLY
Summer 1975, 17,(2): 164-174.

Bruch, Catherine B.
For identification of the disadvantaged gifted.
THE GIFTED CHILD QUARTERLY
1971, Winter, 267-272.

Burt, Cyril
THE GIFTED CHILD
Great Britain: Hodder & Stoughton, 1975.

Burton, William H., Roland B. Kimball, & Richard L.
Wing
EDUCATION FOR EFFECTIVE THINKING
Appleton-Century-Crofts, Inc., 1960.

Canfield, J. & Wells, H.C.
100 WAYS TO ENHANCE SELF-CONCEPT IN THE
CLASSROOM: A HANDBOOK FOR TEACHERS AND PARENTS
Englewood Cliffs, New Jersey: Prentice-Hall, 1976.

Cattell, R.
The structure of intelligence in relation to the nature-nurture
controversy. R. Cancro (ed), INTELLIGENCE: GENETIC
AND ENVIRONMENTAL INFLUENCES
New York: Grune & Stratton, 1971.

Clark, Barbara
GROWING UP GIFTED
Columbus: Charles M. Merrill Publishing Company, 1979.

Cline, Starr
Simulation: A teaching strategy for the gifted and talented.
THE GIFTED CHILD QUARTERLY
Summer 1979, 23 (2):   269-283.

Correll, Marsha M.
TEACHING THE GIFTED AND TALENTED
Bloomington, Ind.: Phi Delta Kappa Educational Foundation,
1978.

Cutts, Norman E. & Nicholas Mosely
TEACHING THE BRIGHT AND GIFTED
Englewood Cliffs, New Jersey: Prentice-Hall, 1957.

DeHaan, R.F.
Essentials of a talent development program. WORKING WITH
SUPERIOR STUDENTS Shertzer (ed)
Chicago: Science Research Associates, 1960.

DeHaan, Robert F.
ACCELERATED LEARNING PROGRAMS
New York: The Center for Applied Research in Education, 1963.

DeHaan, Robert F.
Identifying Gifted Children. SOCIAL SERVICE REVIEW
March 1957, 65: 41-48.

DeHaan, Robert F. & Robert J. Havighurst
EDUCATING GIFTED CHILDREN
Chicago: University of Chicago, 1961.

Drevdahl, John E.
Factors of importance for creativity. JOURNAL OF
CLINICAL PSYCHOLOGY
January 1956.

Dunn, Hoyd M.
EXCEPTIONAL CHILDREN IN THE SCHOOLS
New York: Holt, Rinehart, & Winston, Inc., 1973.

Durr, William K.
THE GIFTED STUDENT
New York: Oxford University Press, 1964.

Engle, T.L.
PSYCHOLOGY: ITS PRINCIPLES AND APPLICATIONS
New York: Harcourt, Brace & World, Inc., 1964.

EPC EDUCATION OF THE GIFTED
Educational Policies Commission, Washington D.C.
National Education Association, 1950.

Feldhusen, J.F. & Treffinger, D.J.
CREATIVE THINKING AND PROBLEM SOLVING IN GIFTED
EDUCATION
Dubuque, Iowa: Kendall/Hunt, 1977.

Ferguson, M.
THE BRAIN REVOLUTION
New York: Taplinger, 1973.

Findley, Warren G. & Miriam M. Bryan
ABILITY GROUPING: 1970 STATUS, IMPACT, AND
ALTERNATIVES
Athens, Ga., Center for Educational Improvement, 1970.

Fine, Benjamin
UNDERACHIEVERS: HOW THEY CAN BE HELPED
New York, E.P. Dutton & Co., Inc., 1967.

Fliegler, Louis A.
CURRICULUM PLANNING FOR THE GIFTED
Englewood Cliffs, New Jersey: Prentice-Hall Inc., 1961.

Fliegler, Louis A. & Charles E. Bish
SUMMARY OF RESEARCH ON THE ACADEMICALLY
TALENTED STUDENT
Washington D.C.: National Education Association of the United
States, 1959.

Fredrickson, Ronald H.
RECOGNIZING AND ASSISTING MULTIPOTENTIAL YOUTH
Columbus, Ohio: Charles E. Merrill Publishing Co., 1972.

Freehill, Maurice F.
GIFTED CHILDREN
New York: The Macmillan Company, 1961.

French, Joseph L.
EDUCATING THE GIFTED
New York: Holt, Rinehart, & Winston, 1959.

Bibliography 100

Gallagher, James J.
Peer acceptance of highly gifted children in elementary school.
ELEMENTARY SCHOOL JOURNAL 58
May 1958, pp. 465-70.

Gallagher, James J.
RESEARCH SUMMARY ON GIFTED CHILD EDUCATION
State of Illinois: Office of the Superintendent of Public Instruction, 1966.

Gallagher, James J.
TEACHING THE GIFTED CHILD
Boston: Allyn & Bacon, 1964, 1976.

Galloway, C.
PSYCHOLOGY FOR LEARNING AND TEACHING
New York: McGraw-Hill, 1976.

Galton, Francis
Hereditary genius. SOME REFLECTIONS ON GENIUS AND OTHER ESSAYS. Brain (ed.)
Philadelphia: J.B. Lippincott Company, 1960.

Gazzanigna, M.S.
THE BISECTED BRAIN
New York: Appleton-Century-Crofts, 1970.

George, W.C.
The third D: Development of talent (Fast-math classes).
NEW VOICES IN COUNSELING THE GIFTED. Colangelo, N. & Zaffran, R.T. (eds).
Dubuque, Iowa: Kendall/Hunt, 1979.

Gold, Milton J.
EDUCATION OF THE INTELLECTUALLY GIFTED
Columbus: Charles E. Merrill Books, Inc., 1965.

Good, Carter V.
DICTIONARY OF EDUCATION
3rd ed. New York: McGraw-Hill Book Company, 1973.

Good, T.L. & J.E. Brophy
EDUCATIONAL PSYCHOLOGY: A REALISTIC APPROACH
New York: Holt, Rinehart, & Winston, 1977.

Gottlieb, David & Charles E. Ramsey
UNDERSTANDING CHILDREN OF POVERTY
Chicago: Science Research Associates, 1967.

Gowan, J.D.
The education of disadvantaged gifted youth.
CALIFORNIA JOURNAL FOR INSTRUCTIONAL IMPROVEMENT
December 1969, pp. 239-251.

Gowan, J.C. & Bruch, C.B.
THE ACADEMICALLY TALENTED STUDENT AND GUIDANCE
New York: Houghton Mifflin Company, 1971.

Gowan, John C. & Demos, George D.
THE EDUCATION AND GUIDANCE OF THE ABLEST
Chicago, Illinois: Charles C. Thomas, 1964.

Gowan, J.C. & E. Paul Torrance
EDUCATING THE ABLEST
Itasco, Illinois: F.E. Peacock, 1971.

Guilford, J.P.
Intellect and the gifted. THE GIFTED CHILD QUARTERLY
1972, 16:(2).

Guilford, J.P.
THE NATURE OF HUMAN INTELLIGENCE
New York: McGraw-Hill, 1967.

Guilford, J.P.
Three faces of intellect. AMERICAN PSYCHOLOGIST
August 1959, 14: (8) pp. 469-479.

Guilford, J.P.
WAY BEYOND THE I.Q.
Buffalo, New York: Creative Education Foundations, 1977.

Hall, Theodore
GIFTED CHILDREN: THE CLEVELAND STORY
New York: The World Publishing Company, 1956.

Hallman, R.
The commonness of creativity. EDUCATIONAL THEORY
1963, 13: 132-136.

Hammer, E.F.
EXCEPTIONAL CHILDREN AND YOUTH. Meyen, (ed.)
Denver, Col.: Love Publishing Company, 1978.

Hammer, E.F.
HANDBOOK ON INSERVICE EDUCATION. Jacobson, (ed.)
Springfield, IL: Superintendent of Public Instruction, 1967.

Havighurst, Robert J.
Conditions productive of superior children. TEACHERS
COLLEGE RECORD
April 1961, 62.

Havighurst, Robert J., Eugene Stivers, & Robert F. DeHaan
A SURVEY OF THE EDUCATION OF GIFTED CHILDREN
The Committee on Human Development, The University of Chicago,
Chicago: University of Chicago Press, 1955.

Hildreth, Gertrude H.
INTRODUCTION TO THE GIFTED
New York: McGraw-Hill Book Company, 1966.

Hopke, William E. (ed)
DICTIONARY OF PERSONNEL AND GUIDANCE TERMS
Chicago: J.G. Ferguson Publishing Co., 1968.

Hurlock, Elizabeth B.
ADOLESCENT DEVELOPMENT
New York: McGraw-Hill, 1957.

Jarecky, Roy K.
Identification of the socially gifted.
EXCEPTIONAL CHILDREN.   May 1959, 25:(8) 415-419.

Johnson, D.W.
REACHING OUT: INTERPERSONAL EFFECTIVENESS AND
SELF-ACTUALIZATION
Englewood Cliffs, N.J.:   Prentice-Hall, 1972.

Kaplan, S.N.
PROVIDING PROGRAMS FOR THE GIFTED AND TALENTED:
A HANDBOOK
Reston, VA: The Council for Exceptional Children, 1977.

Khatena, J.
THE CREATIVELY GIFTED CHILD
New York: Vantage Press, 1978.

Kirk, Samuel A.
EDUCATING EXCEPTIONAL CHILDREN
Boston: Houghton Mifflin Co., 1972.

Kretschmer
The Psychology of Men of Genius. SOME REFLECTIONS
ON GENIUS AND OTHER ESSAYS Brain (ed.)
Philadelphia: J.B.& Lippincott Company, 1960.

Kuo, You-Yuh
TEACHING STRATEGIES FOR DEVELOPING INTELLECTUAL
ABILITIES
Muncie, Indiana: The East-West Culture Exchange, 1976.

Bibliography   104

L'Abate, Luciano & Leonard T. Curtis
TEACHING THE EXCEPTIONAL CHILD
Philadelphia: W.B. Saunders Co.   1975.

Lawson, J.D., L.J. Griffin, F.D. Donant
LEADERSHIP IS EVERYBODY'S BUSINESS
San Luis Obispo, California: Impact Publishers, 1971.

Laycock, S.P.
GIFTED CHILDREN: A HANDBOOK FOR THE CLASSOOM
Vancouver: The Copp Clark Publishing Co., 1967.

Lazerson, Arlyne
PSYCHOLOGY TODAY: AN INTRODUCTION
New York: Random House, Inc., 1975.

Leeper, Sarah Hammond
GOOD SCHOOLS FOR YOUNG CHILDREN
New York: Macmillan Publishing Company, 1974.

MacKinnon, Donald W.
The nature and nurture of creative talent. AMERICAN
PSYCHOLOGIST 1962, 17:484-495.

Leese, J. & Fliegler, L.A.
Problems and practices. CURRICULUM AND PLANNING
FOR THE GIFTED. Fliegler, (ed.)
Englewood Cliffs, New Jersey: Prentice-Hall, 1961.

Maeroff, Gene I.
The unfavored gifted few. READINGS IN EDUCATION.
ANNUAL EDITION, 78/79 Schultz, (ed.)
Guilford, Ct.: Dushkin, 1978.

Maker, C. June
PROVIDING PROGRAMS FOR THE GIFTED HANDICAPPED
Reston, Virginia: Council for Exceptional Children, 1977.

Malone, Charlotte E.
Potential Abilities: To Preserve and To Enhance. THE GIFTED CHILD QUARTERLY Summer 1975, 19:(2), 161-163.

Marland, S., Jr.
EDUCATION OF THE GIFTED AND TALENTED Report to the Congress of the United States by the U.S. Commissioner of Education.
Washington, D.C.: U.S. Government Printing Office, 1972.

Martinson, Ruth A.
THE IDENTIFICATION OF THE GIFTED AND TALENTED Reston, Va: Council for Exceptional Children, 1977.

May, R.
The nature of creativity. CREATIVITY AND ITS CULTIVATION New York: Harper & Row, 1959.

McFee, June King
PREPARATION FOR ART (2nd ed.)
California: Wadsworth, 1970.

Meeker, Mary Nacol
THE STRUCTURE OF INTELLECT; ITS INTERPRETATION AND USES
Columbus: Charles E. Merrill Co., 1969.

Mehrens, William A. & Irvin J. Lehmann
MEASUREMENT AND EVALUATION IN EDUCATION AND PSYCHOLOGY 2nd ed.
New York: Holt, Rinehart, & Winston, 1978.

Mehrens, William A. & Irvin J. Lehmann
STANDARDIZED TESTS IN EDUCATION
New York: Holt, Rinehart, & Winston, Inc., 1969.

Meyen, E.L. (ed.)
EXCEPTIONAL CHILDREN AND YOUTH: AN INTRODUCTION
Denver, Colorado: Love Publishing Company, 1978.

Newland, T. Ernest
THE GIFTED AND SOCIOEDUCATIONAL PERSPECTIVE
Englewood Cliffs, New Jersey: Prentice-Hall, 1976.

Noll, Victor H.
INTRODUCTION TO EDUCATIONAL MEASUREMENT (2nd ed.)
Boston: Houghton Mifflin, 1979.

Ornstein, R.E.
THE PSYCHOLOGY OF CONSCIOUSNESS
San Francisco: W.H. Freeman, 1972.

Osborn, A.
EXCEPTIONAL CHILDREN AND YOUTH.   Meyen (ed.)
Denver, Colorado: Love Publishing Company, 1978.

Otto, Henry J.
CURRICULUM ENRICHMENT FOR GIFTED ELEMENTARY
SCHOOL CHILDREN IN REGULAR CLASSES
Austin, Texas: The University of Texas, 1955.

Owen, Steven, H. Parker Blount, & Henry Moscow
EDUCATIONAL PSYCHOLOGY: AN INTRODUCTION
Boston: Little, Brown, & Company, 1978.

Parnes, S.
CREATIVE BEHAVIOR GUIDEBOOK
New York: Charles Scribner's Sons, 1967.

Passow, A.H.
Enrichment of education for the gifted. EDUCATION FOR
THE GIFTED: Fifty-seventh Yearbook of the National Society
for the Study of Education, Part II, N.B. Henry (ed.)
Chicago: University of Chicago Press, 1958.

Passow, A. Harry & Miriam L. Goldberg
The gifted. BEHAVIORAL RESEARCH ON EXCEPTIONAL
CHILDREN Washington, D.C.: The Council for Exceptional
Children, NEA, 1963.

Payne, David A.
THE ASSESSMENT OF LEARNING
Lexington, Mass: D.C. Heath & Company, 1974.

Perkins, H.V.
HUMAN DEVELOPMENT AND LEARNING 2nd edition.
Belmont, California: Wadsworth Publishing Company, 1974.

Plowman, P. & J.P. Rice
FINAL REPORT: CALIFORNIA PROJECT TALENT
Sacramento, California: State Department of Education, 1969.

Prince, G.M.
THE PRACTICE OF CREATIVITY
New York: Harper & Row, 1970.

Pulaski, J.A.S.
UNDERSTANDING PIAGET: AN INTRODUCTION TO
CHILDREN'S COGNITIVE DEVELOPMENT
New York: Harper & Row, 1971.

Radcliffe, S. & W. Hatch
ADVANCED STANDING: NEW DIMENSIONS IN HIGHER
EDUCATION (No. 8).
Washington D.C.: U.S. Government Printing Office, 1961.

Raph, J.B., M.L. Goldberg, & A.H. Passow
BRIGHT UNDERACHIEVERS
New York: Teachers College Press, 1966.

Renzulli, J.S.
A GUIDEBOOK FOR EVALUATING PROGRAMS FOR
THE GIFTED AND TALENTED
Ventura, California: Office of the Ventura County
Superintendent of Schools, 1975.

Renzulli, J.S.
Talent potential in minority group students. EXCEPTIONAL
CHILDREN.
1973, 39:(6), 437-444.

Renzulli, J.S.
THE ENRICHMENT TRIAD MODEL: A GUIDE FOR DEVELOPING
DEFENSIBLE PROGRAMS FOR THE GIFTED AND TALENTED
Wethersfield, Connecticut: Creative Learning Press, 1977.

Renzulli, Joseph S.
What makes giftedness?   Re-examining a Definition.   PHI
DELTA KAPPAN.
November 1978, pp. 180-184, 261.

Rhodes, M.
An analysis of creativity.   PHI DELTA KAPPAN
1961, 42: 305-310.

Rice, J.P.
THE GIFTED: DEVELOPING TOTAL TALENT
Springfield, Illinois: Charles C. Thomas, 1970.

Riessman, Frank
THE CULTURALLY DEPRIVED CHILD
New York: Harper & Row, 1962.

Robb, G.P., L.C. Bernardoni & R.W. Johnson.
ASSESSMENT OF INDIVIDUAL MENTAL ABILITY
San Francisco: Intext Educational Publishers, 1972.

Rogers, C.
Toward a theory of creativity. CREATIVITY AND ITS
CULTIVATION
New York: Harper & Row, 1959.

Russell, David
CHILDREN'S THINKING
Ginn & Company, (Blaisdell Publishing Company) 1956.

Sato, I.S.
The Culturally Different Gifted Child - the Dawning of His
Day? EXCEPTIONAL CHILDREN. 1974, 40: pp. 572-583.

Sax, G.
PRINCIPLES OF EDUCATIONAL AND PSYCHOLOGICAL
MEASUREMENT AND EVALUATION
Belmont, California: Wadsworth Publishing Company, 1980.

Skinner, Charles E.
EDUCATIONAL PSYCHOLOGY
New Jersey: Prentice-Hall, 1959.

SPECIAL EDUCATION REGULATIONS AND PROCEDURES
Georgia Department of Education, 1975.

Stanley, J., D. Keating, & L. Fox. (eds.)
MATHEMATICAL TALENT: DISCOVERY, DESCRIPTION, AND
DEVELOPMENT
Baltimore: Johns Hopkins University Press, 1974.

Stufflebeam, D.L. et al.
EDUCATIONAL EVALUATION AND DECISION-MAKING
Bloomington, Ind.: Phi Delta Kappan, 1971.

Suchman, J. Richard
Inquiry training in the elementary school. SCIENCE TEACHER
November, 1960, pp. 42-47.

Bibliography 110

Sumption, Merle R. & Evelyn M. Leucking
EDUCATION OF THE GIFTED
New York: The Ronald Press Company, 1960.

Suran, Bernard G. & Joseph Rizzo
SPECIAL CHILDREN: AN INTEGRATIVE APPROACH
Glenview, Illinois: Scott, Foresman, & Company, 1979.

Syphers, D.F.
GIFTED AND TALENTED CHILDREN: PRACTIAL
PROGRAMMING FOR TEACHERS AND PRINCIPALS
Reston, Virignia: Council for Exceptional Children, 1972.

Taylor, C.W.
Be talent developers as well as knowledge dispensers.
TODAY'S EDUCATION
1968, 57:   (9), 67-69.

Taylor, C.W.
Clues to creative teaching: The creative process and education.
INSTRUCTOR
1963, 73:   4-5.

Taylor, C.W.
The creative individual: A new portrait in giftedness.
EDUCATIONAL LEADERSHIP
1960, 18:   7-12.

Thompson, M.
Identifying the gifted.   THE NATIONAL ELEMENTARY
PRINCIPAL
1972, 51:   (5), 37-44.

Thorndike, Robert L.
MEASUREMENT AND EVALUATION IN PSYCHOLOGY AND
EDUCATION
New York: John Wiley & Sons, Inc., 1969.

Torrance, E.P. & R.E. Meyers
CREATIVE LEARNING AND TEACHING
New York: Harper & Row, 1970.

Torrance, E. Paul
EDUCATION AND THE CREATIVE POTENTIAL
Minneapolis: The University of Minnesota Press, 1963.

Torrance, E. Paul
GIFTED CHILDREN IN THE CLASSROOM
New York: The Macmillan Company, 1965.

Torrance, E.P.
Non-test indicators of creative talent among disadvantaged
children. THE GIFTED CHILD QUARTERLY
1973, 7: (1), pp. 5-8.

Torrance, E. Paul
Non-test ways of identifying the gifted. THE GIFTED CHILD
QUARTERLY
1962, pp. 71-75.

Torrance, E. Paul & Salah Mourad
Role of Hemisphericity in Performance on Selected Measures
of Creativity. THE GIFTED CHILD QUARTERLY
Spring 1979, 23:(1), 44-54.

Treffinger, Donald J.
Teaching for Self-Directed Learning: A Priority for the Gifted
and Talented. THE GIFTED CHILD QUARTERLY
19:(1), 46-59.

Walker, J.J.
The gifted and talented. EXCEPTIONAL CHILDREN AND YOUTH:
AN INTRODUCTION. Meyen (ed.)
Denver, Colorado: Love Publishing Company, 1978.

Ward, Virgil
THE GIFTED STUDENT: A MANUAL FOR PROGRAM
IMPROVEMENT
A Report of the Southern Regional Project for Education
of the Gifted. 1962.

WEBSTER'S NEW WORLD DICTIONARY
Nashville, Tenn.: The Southwestern Company, 1968.

Wechsler, D.
THE MEASUREMENT AND APPRAISAL OF ADULT
INTELLIGENCE 4th edition.
Baltimore: Williams & Wilkins, 1958.

White, Alan J.
TASK FORCE REPORT ON CURRICULUM
Hartford, Connecticut. 1978.

Whitmore, J.R.
GIFTEDNESS, CONFLICT, AND UNDERACHIEVEMENT
Boston: Allyn & Bacon, 1980.

Williams, F.E.
IDENTIFYING AND MEASURING CREATIVE POTENTIAL
Volume I.
Englewood Cliffs, N.J.: Educational Technology
Publications, 1972.

Williams, Frank E.
CLASSROOM IDEAS FOR ENCOURAGING THINKING AND
FEELING
Buffalo, NY: D.O.K. Publishers, Inc., 1970.

Wilson, John A. Mildred C. Robeck, & William B. Michael
PSYCHOLOGICAL FOUNDATIONS OF LEARNING AND
TEACHING
New York: McGraw-Hill, Inc., 1967.

Witty, Paul A.
Some considerations in the education of gifted children.
EDUCATIONAL ADMINISTRATION AND SUPERVISION.
1940, 26: 512-521.

Worcester, D.A.
THE EDUCATION OF CHILDREN OF ABOVE AVERAGE
MENTALITY
Lincoln: University of Nebraska Press, 1956.

ASSOCIATIONS

AMERICAN ASSOCIATION FOR GIFTED CHILDREN, THE

The American Association for Gifted Children, the first voluntary non-profit organization in the United States devoted exclusively to the needs of gifted, talented, and creative children, was founded in 1946 by Dr. Ruth Strang and Miss Pauline Williamson. The Association assists in developing special materials for parents and community leaders and in encouraging studies, conferences, scholarships, and other services related to the development of the gifted. Annual membership dues are $15.00.
Contact:
Marjorie L. Craig
Vice President and Executive Director
15 Gramercy Park
New York, NY 10003
(212) 473-4266

NATIONAL ASSOCIATION FOR GIFTED CHILDREN

National Association for Gifted Children is an organization of educators, parents, and community people interested in the development of gifted people. The Association serves as a communication network for people seeking information related to giftedness. The Association publishes several books and pamphlets as well as a quarter journal and newsletter. Annual subscription: $26.00
Address:
5100 N. Edgewood Drive
St. Paul MN 55112
(612) 784-3475

NATIONAL/STATE LEADERSHIP TRAINING INSTITUTE ON THE GIFTED AND THE TALENTED (N/S-LTI-G/T)

N/S-LTI-G/T is an Institute that was established in response to the U.S. Office of Education Commissioner's Report to Congress in 1971 to "upgrade supervisory personnel and program planning for the gifted at the state level." Since the Institute has been in existence it has assisted regional, state, intermediate and local education agencies to plan, initiate, and extend appropriate educational programs for gifted and talented students. In addition, technical assistance is offered in the areas of curriculum development, instructional strategies, assessment procedures, evaluation, program planning/expansion, and special areas such as culturally different, the arts/creativity, and parents of gifted/talented. A monthly BULLETIN is also published. Subscription: $13.50. Director: Irving S. Sato

National Institute on the Gifted and the Talented
316 West Second Street, PH-C
Los Angeles, CA 90012
(213) 489-7470

OFFICE OF THE GIFTED AND TALENTED (OGT)

The Office of the Gifted and Talented coordinated federal leadership in education of the gifted and talented. The office has been closed, at least temporarily.

THE ASSOCIATION FOR THE GIFTED (TAG)

The Association for the Gifted (TAG) is a division of the Council for Exceptional Children (CEC). For membership information write: The Association for the Gifted, Council for Exceptional Children, 1920 Association Drive, Reston, VA 22091. (703) 620-3660.

WORLD COUNCIL FOR GIFTED & TALENTED CHILDREN

The World Council for Gifted and Talented Children is an international organization designed to promote the educational and developmental well-being of gifted and talented children throughout the world. It serves as a medium of exchange of ideas, program plans, research, curriculum, and publications. The World Council is directed by an Executive composed of members from different countries, and served by a Secretariat centered at Teachers College, Columbia University, New York. It publishes a quarterly newsletter and a semi-annual journal. Dues are $30.00 a year and include the newsletter and journal. Address:

World Council for Gifted & Talented Children
Box 218
Teachers College, Columbia University
525 W 120th St
New York, NY   10027
(212) 678-3866.

Appendix C

JOURNALS AND PUBLICATIONS

EXCEPTIONAL CHILDREN

Official journal of The Council for Exceptional Children. The journal is published 8 times a year, September through May, excluding December. Member's dues to the Council for Exceptional Children include a subscription to EXCEPTIONAL CHILDREN. Single copy price is $3.50. Without membership: U.S. $20.00 per year; Canada, PUSA. and all other countries, $22.00.
Director: M. Angele Thomas
            Council for Exceptional Children
            1920 Association Drive
            Reston, Virginia   22091

G/C/T

A magazine for parents and teachers of gifted, creative, and talented children published 5 times per year by G/C/T Publishing Company, Box 66654, Mobile, Alabama 36606. Subscription rate: $17.50 per year.
Editor/Publisher: Marvin J. Gold

GIFTED CHILDREN NEWSLETTER

A monthly newsletter for parents of gifted children and other concerned persons. Subscription: $24.00.
Editor: James Alvino
        Gifted Children Newsletter
        Box 115
        Sewell NJ   08080

GIFTED CHILD QUARTERLY, THE (GCQ)

The GIFTED CHILD QUARTERLY, the official publication of the National Association for Gifted Children (NAGC), is published quarterly by NAGC, 217 Gregory Drive, Hot Springs, Arkansas 71901.

The QUARTERLY provides an open forum for the development, exchange, and analysis of knowledge relating to gifted persons. It is intended for audiences of professional educators and administrators, researchers and theorists, and concerned lay persons.

Single issues are available for $5.00. NAGC member dues of $20.00 include a subscription to GCO.

Editor: Donald J. Treffinger
160 Monroe Drive
Williamsville, NY 14221

GIFTED INTERNATIONAL

The Journal for the World Council for Gifted and Talented Children. Its purpose is to foster an international exchange of ideas, research findings, theories, programs, and information. Published twice a year. Subscription $12.00; single copies $7.00

Editor: Dr. Dorothy Sisk
Department of Education
University of South Florida
Tampa FL   33620

JOURNAL FOR THE EDUCATION OF THE GIFTED (JEG)

The Journal for the Education of the Gifted, published quarterly, is the official publication of The Association for the Gifted (TAG), 1920 Association Drive, Reston, Virginia 22091. Member's dues to TAG include a subscription to JEG. Annual subscription for non-members: $12.00. Institutional subscriptions: $20.00. Single copy price: $3.50. Subscribers outside the United States add $1.50.

Editor: Kenneth Seeley
University of Denver
School of Education
Denver CO 80208

JOURNAL OF CREATIVE BEHAVIOR

A quarterly journal published by the Creative Education Foundation, Inc. Subscriptions: $10.00 per year. Address inquiries to the Managing Editor, Journal of Creative Behavior, State University College at Buffalo, 1300 Elmwood Avenue, Buffalo, New York 14222.

TAG UPDATE

TAG UPDATE is issued five times annually and is the official newsletter of The Association for the Gifted, a division of the Council for Exceptional Children. Annual subscription for non-members of CEC and TAG: $10.00.

Editor: James Delisle
Box U7
Univ of Connecticut
Storrs Ct   06268

TESTS

ACADEMIC PROMISE TEST (APT)
Authors: G.K. Bennett, M.G. Bennet, D.M. Clendennon, J.E.
Doppelt, J.H. Ricks, Jr., H.G. Seashore, and A.G. Wesman

   A group test designed to provide a broad, differential
description of the academic abilities of students in grades 6 -
9. The APT battery consists of four tests: Verbal, Numerical,
Abstract Reasoning, and Language Usage. The test may be
hand-scored or machine scored. Scoring services are also
available from the publisher.

   Robb, Bernardoni, & Johnson, 1972, 296-8.

CALIFORNIA TEST OF MENTAL MATURITY (CTMM)
Long Form, 1963 Revision
Authors: E.T. Sullivan, W.W. Clark, and E.W. Tiegs

   A group test of abilities designed to provide information
about the functional capacities that are basic to learning,
problem-solving, and responding to new situations. Test is
organized around five factors: logical reasoning, numerical
reasoning, verbal concepts, memory and spatial relations. The
levels of the Long Form are: O - grade range K-1; 1 - grade
range 1-3; 2 - grade range 4-6; 3 - grade range 7-8; 4 - grade
range 9-12; and 5 - grade range 12-Adult. Contains twelve
subtests grouped into a Language and Non-Language Section. May
be handscored or machine scored. The publisher provides
deviation IQ, mental age, standard score and percentile norms
for the section and total scores. Standard score and percentile
norms are provided for the factor scores. Available from:
California Test Bureau (See Appendix E).

   Robb, Bernardoni, & Johnson, 1972, 289-291.

CALIFORNIA TEST OF MENTAL MATURITY (CTMM)
Short Form, 1963 Revision
Authors: E.T. Sullivan, W.W. Clark, and E.W. Tiegs

The group test which consists of seven test units, each of which presumably measures ability in a manner different from the others. The seven test units are grouped according to four factors, and the items are all of the multiple-choice type. The four factors are: logical reasoning, numerical reasoning, verbal concepts, and memory. Time requirements vary from 39 to 43 minutes actual testing time, depending on the level being used.
The levels of the Short Form are: O - grade range k-L1: 1 - grade range H1-3: 1H - grade range 3-4: 2 - grade range 4-6; 2H - grade range 6-7: 3 - grade range 7-8: 4 - grade range 9-12:, and 5 - grade range 12 - adult.   Available from: California Test Bureau (see Appendix E).
Robb, Bernardoni, & Johnson, 1972, 289-291.

THE HENMON-NELSON TESTS OF MENTAL ABILITY
(1972 Revision)
Authors: T.A. Lamke and M.J. Nelson

Group intelligence tests. Primary Battery (grades K-2) and Form 1 (Grades 3-12). The Primary Battery has three separate subtests: a Listening Test, (general information), a Picture Vocabulary Test, and a Size and Number Test. Instructions and test questions are given orally, so reading skill does not influence test performance. There are three levels (3-6, 6-9, and 9-12) for Form 1. The overlap provides a choice when testing in grades 6 and 9. For both the Primary Battery and Form 1 the manuals provide DIQs for each age group; stanines and percentile ranks of DIQs; and stanines and percentile ranks of raw scores by grade. Available from: Houghton Mifflin (See Appendix E).
Mehrens & Lehmann, 1978, 434.

LORGE-THORNDIKE INTELLIGENCE TEST
Authors: I. Lorge, R.L. Thorndike, and E. Hagen

Group test designed to measure abstract intelligence, which is defined as "the ability to work with ideas and the relationships among ideas" (Lorge, Thorndike, and Hagen, 1966, p. 1). Available in two forms: A and B for Primary Batteries and 1 and 2 for Multilevel Edition.

The Multilevel Edition of the Lorge-Thorndike Intelligence Test provides both a Verbal and Nonverbal Battery, for grades 3-13, in a single booklet. There is a graded series of items divided into eight separate scales for use within this grade range. The Verbal Battery consists of five subtests which contain only verbal items. The subtests are: Vocabulary, Verbal Classification, Sentence Completion, Arithmetic Reasoning, and Verbal Analogy. The Nonverbal Battery is composed of items which are either pictorial or numerical. The items are arranged to form three subjects: Pictorial Classification, Pictorial Analogy, and Numerical Relationships. According to the test authors, the Nonverbal Battery yields an estimate of scholastic aptitude relatively independent of reading ability.

There is no time limit set for the Primary Batteries. The Verbal Battery of the Multilevel Edition requires a total of 35 minutes of actual testing time; the Nonverbal Battery requires 25 minutes. Available from: Houghton Mifflin Company (See Appendix E).

Robb, Bernardoni & Johnson, 1972, 292-294.

METROPOLITAN ACHIEVEMENT TESTS
Authors: W.N. Durost, H.H. Bixler, G.H. Hildreth, K.W. Lund, J.W. Wrightstone, W.H. Evans, J.D. Leake, H.A. Bowman, C. Cosgrove and J.G. Read

A group achievement test series at six levels: Primary I Battery - Grade 1.5; Primary II Battery - Grade 2; Elementary Battery - Grades 3-4; Intermediate Battery - Grades 5-6; Advanced Battery - Grades 7-9; and High School - Grades 9-12.

The test was designed to measure achievement on what was determined to be the material to which students were most commonly exposed. It relfects the emphasis schools place on rote learning of information and skills, and therefore does not measure higher cognitive processes. The tests at all levels make possible the measure of superior achievement, although measurement of poor learner is generally inadequate. National norms are provided, although test users are encouraged to develop their own local norms, stanines, and percentile ranks. Available from: Harcourt, Brace, Jovanovich (See Appendix E).
Clark, 1979, 415-416.

OTIS-LENNON MENTAL ABILITY TEST
Authors: A.S. Otis and R.T. Lennon

A group intelligence test which is timed and claims to be a power measure for grades K-12. Scores may be given as deviation IQs, as age and grade percentile ranks showing the pupils' standing in the national sample, and as stanines. The Otis-Lennon seeks to test the verbal educational aspects of mental abilities, not the practical mechanical, and items measure road reasoning abilities involving manipulation of ideas. The test has six levels: grades K, 1-1.5, 1.6-3.9, 4-6, 7-9, and 10-12. Available from Harcourt, Brace, and Jovanovich (See Appendix E).
Clark, 1979, 414.

PEABODY PICTURE VOCABULARY TEST
Author: Lloyd M. Dunn

An untimed individual test with two forms, A and B, for ages 2.5-18. It gives a percentile rank, MA, or IQ score. It is designed to measure verbal intelligence. Test is administered by reading stimulus words to a subject who is viewing a card where several line drawings are shown. The subject then indicates which picture best illustrates the word given. It takes approximately 15 minutes to give. Service,

Inc. (See Appendix E)
                Clark, 1979, 408.

SLOSSON INTELLIGENCE TEST
Author: R. Slosson

A brief individual test of intelligence designed to be used with infants from two weeks through adults (27 years). There are no time limits. Gives a ratio IQ score. Testing and scoring take from 10-30 minutes and can be used by relatively untrained examiners. Infant testing items assess postural control and locomotion. Between 2 and 4 years, the emphasis is on language skills. Above 4 years, all questions are presented verbally and require spoken responses. Content includes mathematical reasoning, vocabulary, auditory memory, and information. Available from Slosson Educational Publications. (See Appendix E).
                Clark, 1979, 409.

STANFORD-BINET INTELLIGENCE SCALE (S-B) - THIRD REVISION

Authors: L.M. Terman and M.A. Merrill
An individual test of mental activities that are known as general intelligence for ages 2 and over. There are few time limits, and when there are, they are generous enough for most subjects to respond. Verbal, nonverbal, and performance items are found in the Binet battery. The test is given orally, scored manually, and the complete test takes from 60-90 minutes to administer. The test requires a trained examiner. Available from: Houghton Mifflin Co. (See Appendix E).
                Clark, 1979, 409.

TORRANCE TEST OF CREATIVE THINKING (FIGURAL AND VERBAL) - TTCT
Author: E. Paul Torrance

A series of verbal and figural tasks requiring thinking analogous to that involved in recognized creative activities. The Verbal Tests require students to ask questions about pictures, suggest how an object can be improved, and imagine outcomes of an improbable situation. The Figural Tests require students to complete open drawings, construct new pictures, and elaborate common shapes. The Verbal Tests can be administered to class-size groups from Grade 4 through graduate school, and as individual tests from kindergarten through Grade 3. Figural Tests may be given to class-size groups for Grade 4 and above and to groups of about half class-size for kindergarten through Grade 4. All tests have ample time limits, so they are not considered speeded. Working time is 45 minutes on the Verbal Test and 30 minutes on the Figural Test. Scores for fluency, flexibility, originality, and elaboration are determined by comparing pupils' responses to comprehensive, detailed scoring guides. The new streamlined scoring of the figural forms includes scoring on five norm-referenced and thirteen criterion-referenced indicators of creativity along with a Creativity Index. Available from: Scholastic Testing Service. (See Appendix E)
Torrance

WECHSLER INTELLIGENCE SCALE FOR CHILDREN -Revised (WISC-R)
Author: David Wechsler

An individual test of mental activities which are known as general intelligence of ages 5-15. The WISC-R gives 15 scores, divided into two scales: verbal and performance. Total score MA and IQ scores are also given. The complete test takes from 40-60 minutes. The IQ equivalency of the 98% score on the WISC-R is 131. This test requires a trained examiner. Available from: Psychological Corporation. (See Appendix E)
Clark, 1979, 411.

TEST PUBLISHERS

American Guidance Service, Inc.
Publisher's Building
Circle Pines, Minnesota   55014

California Test Bureau
Del Monte Research Park
Monterey, California   93940

Harcourt, Brace, Jovanovich
757 3rd Avenue
Test Department
New York, New York   10017

Houghton Mifflin Company
110 Tremont Street
Boston, Massachusetts   02107

The Psychological Corporation
304 East 45th Street
New York, New York   10017

Scholastic Testing Services
480 Meyer Road
Bensonville IL 60106

Slosson Educational Publications, Inc.
140 Pine Street
East Aurora, New York   14052

SOI Institute
343 Richmond Street
El Segundo, California   90245

ACKNOWLEDGMENTS

The authors and publisher of The Dictionary of Gifted, Talented, and Creative Education Terms wish to thank the following authors and publishers for permission to use quotations from their publications:

AMERICAN PSYCHOLOGICAL ASSOCIATION, Arlington, Virginia:
From Three Faces of Intellect by J.P. Guilford in AMERICAN PSYCHOLOGIST, August 1959, 14 (8), 469-479; reprinted by permission of the publisher.
From The Nature and Nurture of Creative Talent by Donald W. MacKinnon in AMERICAN PSYCHOLOGIST, 1962, 17, 484-495; reprinted by permission of the publisher.

ASSOCIATION FOR SUPERVISION AND CURRICULUM DEVELOPMENT, Alexandria, Virginia:
From The Creative Individual: A New Portrait in Giftedness by Calvin W. Taylor in EDUCATIONAL LEADERSHIP, 1960, 18, 7-12; reprinted with permission of the Association for Supervision and Curriculum Development and Calvin W. Taylor. Copyright (c) 1960 by the Association for Supervision and Curriculum Development. All rights reserved.

ASSOCIATION OF ELEMENTARY PRINCIPALS, Arlington, Virginia:
From NATIONAL ELEMENTARY PRINCIPAL Vol. 51, No. 5, July/August, 1972. Copyright 1972 National Association of Elementary School Principals. All rights reserved.

CALIFORNIA STATE DEPARTMENT OF EDUCATION, Sacramento, California:
From FINAL REPORT: CALIFORNIA PROJECT TALENT by P. Plowman and J.P. Rice. (c) 1969 by the California State Department of Education. Reprinted by permission of the publisher, California State Department of Education.

CENTER FOR EDUCATIONAL IMPROVEMENT, Athens, Georgia:
From ABILITY GROUPING: 1970 STATUS, IMPACT, AND ALTERNATIVES by Warren G. Findley and Miriam M. Bryan, 1970; reprinted by permission of the publisher.

CHARLES C. THOMAS, Springfield, Illinois:
From THE EDUCATION AND GUIDANCE OF THE ABLEST by John C. Gowan and George D. Demos, 1964; reprinted by permission of the publisher.
From DEVELOPING TOTAL TALENT by J.P. Rice, 1970; reprinted by permission of the publisher.

Acknowledgments 128

CHARLES E. MERRILL PUBLISHING COMPANY, Columbus, Ohio:
From GROWING UP GIFTED by Barbara Clark, 1979; reprinted
by permission of the publisher.

From RECOGNIZING AND ASSISTING MULTIPOTENTIAL YOUTH
By Ronald H. Fredrickson and J.W.M. Rothney, 1972; reprinted by
permission of the publisher.
From EDUCATION OF THE INTELLECTUALLY GIFTED by Milton
J. Gold, 1965; reprinted by permission of the publisher.
From THE STRUCTURE OF INTELLECT: ITS INTERPRETATION
AND USES by Mary Nacol Meeker, 1969; reprinted by permission of
the publisher.

CHARLES SCRIBNER'S SONS, New York:
From CREATIVE BEHAVIOR GUIDEBOOK by S. Parnes, 1967;
reprinted by permission of the publisher.

CLINICAL PSYCHOLOGY PUBLISHING CO., INC., Brandon, Vermont:
From Factors of Importance for Creativity by John E. Drevdahl
in JOURNAL OF CLINICAL PSYCHOLOGY, January 1956; reprinted by
permission of the publisher.

COPP CLARK PITMAN, Toronto, Canada:
From Samuel R. Laycock's GIFTED CHILDREN: A HANDBOOK FOR
THE CLASSROOM TEACHER. (c) Copp Clark Publishing, 1957. Repro-
duced with permission from the publisher.

CREATIVE LEARNING PRESS, INC., Weathersfield, Connecticut:
From THE ENRICHMENT TRIAD MODEL: A GUIDE FOR DEVELOPING
PROGRAMS FOR THE GIFTED AND TALENTED by J.S. Renzulli, 1977;
reprinted by permission of the publisher.

CRM BOOKS, A DIVISION OF RANDOM HOUSE, INC., New York, New
York:
From PSYCHOLOGY TODAY: AN INTRODUCTION by Arlyne
Lazerson, (c) 1975; reprinted by permission of the publisher.

D.O.K., Buffalo, New York:
From BALDWIN IDENTIFICATION MATRIX INSERVICE KIT FOR
THE IDENTIFICATION OF GIFTED AND TALENTED STUDENTS
by A. Baldwin and J. Wooster, 1977; reprinted by permission of
the publisher.
From CLASSROOM IDEAS FOR ENCOURAGING THINKING AND FEELING
by Frank E. Williams, 1970; reprinted by permission of the
publisher.

EDUCATIONAL TECHNOLOGY PUBLICATIONS, Englewood Clifs, New
Jersey:
From IDENTFYING AND MEASURING CREATIVE POTENTIAL.
Volume I. Part of the Total Creativity Program of Eleven Volumes
and Components by F.E. Williams, 1972; reprinted by permission of
the publisher.

129 Acknowledgments

EDUCATIONAL THEORY, Urbana, Illinois:
From The Commonness of Creativity by R. Hallman in EDUCATIONAL
THEORY, 13, 1963; reprinted by permission of the publisher.

E.P. DUTTON AND COMPANY, INC., New York, New York:
From UNDERACHIEVERS: HOW THEY CAN BE HELPED by Benjamin
Fine, 1967; reprinted by permission of the publisher.

GINN & COMPANY, Lexington, Massachusetts:
From CHILDREN'S THINKING by David Russell, 1956, reprinted
by permission of the publisher.

GRUNE AND STRATTON, INC., New York, New York:
From Towards a Behavioral Definition of Genius by R.S.
Albert in THE INTELLECTUALLY GIFTED: AN OVERVIEW.
(Dennis & Dennis, eds.) Copyright (c) 1976; reprinted by per-
mission of Grune and Stratton.
From The Structure of Intelligence in Relation to the
Nature-Nurture Controversy by R. Catell in INTELLIGENCE:
GENETIC AND ENVIRONMENTAL INFLUENCES. (Cancro ed.) Copyright
(c) 1971; reprinted by permission of Grune and Stratton.

HARCOURT, BRACE, AND JOVANOVICH, New York, New York:
From THE GIFTED STUDENT AS FUTURE SCIENTIST by P.F.
Brandwein, 1955; reprinted by permission of the publisher.
From PSYCHOLOGY: ITS PRINCIPLES AND APPLICATIONS by
T.L. Engle, 1964; reprinted by permission of the publisher.

HODDER AND STOUGHTON, Great Britain:
From THE GIFTED CHILD by Cyril R. Burt, 1975; reprinted
by permission of the publisher, Hodder and Stoughton.

HOLT, RINEHART AND WINSTON, New York, New York:
From EXCEPTIONAL CHILDREN IN THE SCHOOLS, Second edition,
Lloyd M. Dunn, (ed.) Copyright (c) 1963, 1973 by Holt,
Rinehart and Winston, Inc. Reprinted by permission of the pub-
lisher, Holt, Rinehart and Winston.
From EDUCATING THE GIFTED by Joseph L. French (c) 1959.
Reprinted by permission of the author.
From EDUCATIONAL PSYCHOLOGY: A REALISTIC APPROACH
by Thomas L. Good and Jere E. Brophy. Copyright (c) 1977 by
Holt, Rinehart and Winston. Reprinted by permission of the
publisher, Holt, Rinehart, and Winston.
From STANDARDIZED TESTS IN EDUCATION by William A.
Mehrens and Irving J. Lehmann. Copyright (c) 1969 by Holt,
Rinehart and Winston, Inc. Reprinted by permission of the
publisher Holt, Rinehart, and Winston.

Acknowledgments 130

From MEASUREMENT AND EVALUATION IN EDUCATION AND
PSYCHOLOGY, Second edition by William A. Mehrens and Irving
J. Lehmann. Copyright (c) 1978 by Holt, Rinehart and Winston,
Inc., Reprinted by permission of the publisher Holt, Rinehart
and Winston.
From TEACHING THE EXCEPTIONAL CHILD by Luciano L'Abate
and Leonard T. Curtis. Copyright (c) 1975 by W.B. Saunders
Company. Reprinted by permission of Holt, Rinehart and Winston.

HOUGHTON MIFFLIN COMPANY, New York, New York:
From J.C. Gowan and C.B. Bruch, THE ACADEMICALLY
TALENTED STUDENT AND GUIDANCE. Copyright, 1971 by Houghton
Mifflin Company. Used by permission.
From Samuel J. Kirk and James J. Gallagher, EDUCATING THE
EXCEPTIONAL CHILDREN Third edition, 1979. Copyright by Houghton
Mifflin Company. Used by permission.
From Noll, Scannell, Craig, INTRODUCTION TO EDUCATIONAL
MEASUREMENT, Fourth edition, 1979. Copyright by Houghton
Mifflin Company. Used by permission.

IMPACT PUBLISHERS, San Luis Obispo, California:
From LEADERSHIP IS EVERYBODY'S BUSINESS by J.D. Lawson,
L.F. Griffin, and F.D. Donant, 1977; reprinted by permission of
the publisher.

J.B. LIPPINCOTT COMPANY, Philadelphia, Pennsylvania:
From SOME REFLECTIONS ON GENIUS AND OTHER ESSAYS by R.
Brain, 1960; reprinted by permission of the publisher.
From The Psychology of Men of Genius by Kretschmer in
SOME REFLECTIONS ON GENIUS AND OTHER ESSAYS (R. Brain, ed.),
1960; reprinted by permission of the publisher.

J.G. FERGUSON PUBLISHING COMPANY, Chicago, Illinois:
From DICTIONARY OF PERSONNEL AND GUIDANCE TERMS, William
E. Hopke, (ed.), 1968; reprinted by permisson of the publisher.

JOHN WILEY AND SONS, New York, New York:
From EDUCATION OF THE GIFTED by Merle R. Sumption and Evelyn
M. Leucking, 1960; reprinted by permission of the publisher.
From MEASUREMENT AND EVALUATION IN PSYCHOLOGY AND
EDUCATION by Robert L. Thorndike, 1969; reprinted by permission
of the publisher.

KENDALL/HUNT, Dubuque, Iowa:
From The Third D: Development of Talent (Fast-Math Classes)
by W.C. George in NEW VOICES IN COUNSELING THE GIFTED.
(Colangelo and Zaffran, eds.), 1979; reprinted by permission of
the publisher.

LITTLE, BROWN AND COMPANY, Boston, Massachusetts:
From EDUCATIONAL PSYCHOLOGY: AN INTRODUCTION by Steven Owen, H. Parker Blount, and Henry Moscow. Copyright (c) 1978 by Little, Brown and Company; reprinted by permission of the publisher and senior author.

MACMILLAN PUBLISHING COMPANY, New York, New York:
From GIFTED CHILDREN IN THE CLASSROOM by E. Paul Torrance. Copyright (c) 1965 by E. Paul Torrance. Reprinted by permission of the publisher and the author.
From GOOD SCHOOLS FOR YOUNG CHILDREN, Third edition by Sarah Hammond Leeper and Dora Sikes Skipper. Copyright (c) 1974 by Macmillan Publishing Co., Inc. Reprinted by permission of the publisher.

MCGRAW-HILL BOOK COMPANY, New York, New York:
From PSYCHOLOGY FOR LEARNING AND TEACHING by C. Galloway. Copyright (c) 1976; reprinted by permission of the publisher.
From DICTIONARY OF EDUCATION (3rd. ed.) by Carter V. Good. Copyright (c) 1973; reprinted by permission of the publisher.
From THE NATURE OF HUMAN INTELLIGENCE by J.P. Guilford. Copyright (c) 1967; reprinted by permission of the publisher.
From INTRODUCTION TO THE GIFTED by Gertrude H. Hildreth. Copyright (c) 1966; reprinted by permission of the publisher.
From ADOLESCENT DEVELOPMENT by Elizabeth B. Hurlock. Copyright (c) 1957; reprinted by permission of the publisher.

NASSP BULLETIN:
From Gifted Programs for the Culturally Different by Ernest M. Bernal, Jr., in the NASSP BULLETIN, March 1976; reprinted by permission of the publisher.

NATIONAL/STATE LEADERSHIP TRAINING INSTITUTE ON THE GIFTED AND TALENTED, Los Angeles, California:
From p. 27 of A GUIDEBOOK FOR EVALUATING PROGRAMS FOR THE GIFTED AND TALENTED (Ventura, California: Office of the Ventura County Superintendent of Schools, 1975). Reprinted by permission of the publisher, The National/State Leadership Training Institute on the Gifted and Talented, 316 West Second Street, Suite PH-C, Los Angeles, California, 90012.

OXFORD UNIVERSITY PRESS, New York, New York:
Excerpted from THE GIFTED STUDENT by William K. Durr. Copyright (c) 1964 by Oxford University Press, Inc. Reprinted by permission.

PHI DELTA KAPPA, Bloomington, Indiana:
From TEACHING THE GIFTED AND TALENTED by Marsha M. Correll (c) 1978; Phi Delta Kappa, Inc.; reprinted by permission of the publisher.

Acknowledgments 132

From EDUCATIONAL EVALUATION AND DECISION-MAKING by
D.L. Stufflebeam et al. (c) 1971, by Phi Delta Kapp, Inc.;
reprinted by permission of the publisher.
From An Analysis of Creativity by Mel Rhodes, in Phi
Delta Kappan, (c) 1961. Phi Delta Kappan, Inc.; reprinted
by permission of the publisher.

PHI DELTA KAPPAN, Bloomington, Indiana:
From What Makes Giftedness? Reexamining a Definition by
Joseph S. Renzulli in PHI DELTA KAPPAN, 1978; copyright (c)
1978 by the author; reprinted by permission of the publisher
and by the author.

PRENTICE-HALL, INC., Englewood Cliffs, New Jersey:
From 100 WAYS TO ENHANCE SELF-CONCEPT IN THE
CLASSROOM: A HANDBOOK FOR TEACHERS AND PARENTS by
Jack Canfield and Harold C. Wells, 1976, p. 1; reprinted by
permission of the publisher.
From TEACHING THE BRIGHT AND GIFTED by Norma E. Cutts
and Nicholas Moseley, 1957, pp. 3, 37; reprinted by permission
of the publisher.
From CURRICULUM PLANNING FOR THE GIFTED by Louis A.
Fliegler, 1961, pp. 16, 18, 25, 27; reprinted by permission of
the publisher.
From REACHING OUT: INTERPERSONAL EFFECTIVENESS AND
SELF-ACTUALIZATION by D.W. Johnson, 1972, pp. 2,3,10,15,18,61,62;
reprinted by permission of the publisher.
From Problems and Practices by J. Leese and L.A. Fliegler in
CURRICULUM AND PLANNING FOR THE GIFTED, (L. Fliegler, ed.),
1961; reprinted by permission of the publisher.
From THE GIFTED IN SOCIOEDUCATIONAL PERSPECTIVE by
Ernest T. Newland, pp. 9,10,24,41,47,63,105,249,251,258,262;
reprinted by permission of the publisher.
From EDUCATIONAL PSYCHOLOGY by Charles E. Skinner, pp. 337,
1959; reprinted by permission of the publisher.

PURDUE RESEARCH FOUNDATION, West Lafayette, Indiana:
From CREATIVE THINKING AND PROBLEM SOLVING IN GIFTED
EDUCATION by John F. Feldhusen and Donald J. Treffinger, 1980;
reprinted by permission of the publisher.

SCIENCE RESEARCH ASSOCIATES, INC., Chicago, Illinois:
From WORKING WITH SUPERIOR STUDENTS: THEORIES AND
PRACTICES (Bruce Shertzer, ed.) (c) 1960, Science Research
Associates, Inc. Reprinted by permission of the publisher.
From UNDERSTANDING CHILDREN OF POVERTY by David Gottlieb
and Charles E. Ramsey. (c) 1967, Science Research Associates,
Inc. Reprinted by permission of the publisher.

SCIENCE TEACHER, THE:
From Inquiry Training in the Elementary School by J. Richard Suchman in THE SCIENCE TEACHER, November 1960; reprinted by permission of the publisher.

SCHOLASTIC TESTING SERVICE, INC., Bensenville, Illinois:
From TORRANCE TESTS OF CREATIVE THINKING (Figural and Verbal) by E. Paul Torrance, 1966; reprinted by permission of the author.

SCOTT, FORESMAN AND COMPANY, Glenview, Illinois:
From SPECIAL CHILDREN: AN INTEGRATED APPROACH by Bernard G. Suran and Joseph V. Rizzo. Copyright (c) 1979 by Scott, Foresman and Company. Reprinted by permission of the publisher.

SOUTHERN REGIONAL EDUCATION BOARD, Atlanta, Georgia:
From THE GIFTED STUDENT: A MANUAL FOR PROGRAM IMPROVEMENT, The Southern Regional Project for the Education of the Gifted by Virgil Ward et al., 1962; reprinted by permission of the publisher.

SPRINGER PUBLISHING COMPANY, New York, New York:
From Howard A. Blatner, ACTING-IN: PRACTICAL APPLICATIONS OF PSYCHODRAMATIC METHODS by Springer Publishing Company, Inc., New York. Used by permission.

STATE OF CONNECTICUT DEPARTMENT OF EDUCATION, Hartford, Connecticut:
From TASK FORCE REPORT ON CURRICULUM by Alan J. White, 1979; reprinted by permission of the publisher.

TEACHERS COLLEGE PRESS, New York, New York:
From J.B. Raph, M.L. Goldberg, and A.H. Passow, BRIGHT UNDERACHIEVERS, 1966; reprinted by permission of the publisher.

TEACHERS COLLEGE RECORD, New York, New York:
From Conditions Productive of Superior Children by Robert J. Havighurst in the TEACHERS COLLEGE RECORD, April 1961; reprinted by permission of the publisher.
THE COUNCIL FOR EXCEPTIONAL CHILDREN, Reston, Virginia:
From Talent Potential in Minority Group Students by J. Renzulli in EXCEPTIONAL CHILDREN, 1973, 39 (6) 437-444. Used by permission.
From Identification of the Socially Gifted by Roy K. Jarecky in EXCEPTIONAL CHILDREN, 1959, 25 (8) 415-419. Used by permission.
From EDUCATIONAL PLANNING FOR THE GIFTED: OVERCOMING CULTURAL, GEOGRAPHIC AND SOCIOECONOMIC BARRIERS (c) 1978; reprinted by permission of the publisher.

Acknowledgments 134

THE EAST-WEST CULTURE EXCHANGE, Muncie, Indiana:
From TEACHING STRATEGIES FOR DEVELOPING INTELLECTUAL
ABILITIES by You-Yuh Kuo, 1976; reprinted by permission of
the author.

THE GIFTED CHILD QUARTERLY, Hot Springs, Arkansas:
Reprinted with permission from Creativity and its Educa-
tional Implications for the Gifted by E. Paul Torrance in THE
GIFTED CHILD QUARTERLY, 1968, 12, 67-78.
Reprinted with permission from Intellect and the Gifted by
J.P. Guilford in THE GIFTED CHILD QUARTERLY, 1972, 16 (2)
Reprinted with permission from Teaching for Self-Directed
Learning: A Priority for the Gifted and Talented by Donald J.
Treffinger in THE GIFTED CHILD QUARTERLY, 1975, 19(1) 46-59.
Reprinted with permission from Role of Hemisphericity in Per-
formance on Selected Sources of Creativity by E. Paul Torrance
and Sulah Mourad in THE GIFTED CHILD QUARTERLY, 1979, 23(1)
44-54.
Reprinted with permission from Non-test Indicators of Creative
Talent among Disadvantaged Children by E.P. Torrance in THE
GIFTED CHILD QUARTERLY, 1962, 71-75.
Reprinted with permission from Simulation: A Teaching Strategy
for the Gifted and Talented by Starr Cline in THE GIFTED
CHILD QUARTERLY, 1979, 23(2) 269-283.
Reprinted with permission from For Identification of the Dis-
advantaged Gifted by C.B. Bruch in THE GIFTED CHILD QUARTERLY,
1971, 267-272.
Reprinted with permission from Assessment of Creativity in
Culturally Different by C.B. Bruch in THE GIFTED CHILD
QUARTERLY, 1975, 19(2) 164-174.

THE JOHNS HOPKINS UNIVERSITY PRESS, Baltimore, Maryland:
From MATHEMATICAL TALENT: DISCOVERY, DESCRIPTION, AND
DEVELOPMENT, edited by J. Stanley, D. Keating, and L. Fox, 1974;
reprinted by permission of the publisher.

THE NATIONAL/STATE LEADERSHIP TRAINING INSTITUTE ON THE
GIFTED AND TALENTED, Los Angeles, California:
From A GUIDEBOOK FOR EVALUATING PROGRAMS FOR THE GIFTED
AND TALENTED by J.S. Renzulli (Ventura, California: Office
of the Ventura County Superintendent of Schools), 1975; re-
printed by permission of the publisher.

THE WORLD PUBLISHING COMPANY, Cleveland, Ohio:
From WEBSTER'S NEW WORLD DICTIONARY, Concise Edition, 1969;
reprinted by permission of the publisher.

THE UNIVERSITY OF CHICAGO PRESS, Chicago, Illinois:
From Enrichment of Education for the Gifted by A.H. Passow
in EDUCATION FOR THE GIFTED. Fifty-seventh Yearbook of the
National Society for the Study of Education, Part II, edited by
N.B. Henry, 1958; reprinted by permission of the publisher.

Reprinted from EDUCATING GIFTED CHILDREN by Robert F. DeHaan and Robert J. Havighurst by permission of The University of Chicago Press.
Reprinted from A SURVEY OF THE EDUCATION OF GIFTED CHILDREN by Robert J. Havighurst, Eugene Strivers and Robert F. DeHaan by permision of the University of Chicago Press.

UNIVERSITY OF MINNESOTA PRESS, Minneapolis, Minnesota:
E. Paul Torrance, EDUCATION AND THE CREATIVE POTENTIAL. Copyright (c) 1963 by the University of Minnesota, University of Minnesota Press, Minneapolis; reprinted by permission of the publisher.

UNIVERSITY OF NEBRASKA PRESS, Lincoln, Nebraska:
Reprinted from THE EDUCATION OF CHILDREN OF ABOVE AVERAGE MENTALITY by D.A. Worcester by permission of University of Nebraska Press. Copyright, 1956, University of Nebraska Press.

U.S. GOVERNMENT PUBLICATIONS, Washington, D.C.:
From EDUCATION OF THE GIFTED AND TALENTED. Report to the Congress of the United States by the U.S. Commissioner of Education, Washington, D.C.: U.S. Government Printing Office, 1972.

VANTAGE PRESS, THE, New York, New York:
From THE CREATIVELY GIFTED CHILD: SUGGESTIONS FOR PARENTS AND TEACHERS by Joe Khatena, New York: Vantage Press, Inc., 1978; reprinted by permission of the publisher.

WADSWORTH PUBLISHING COMPANY, Belmont, California:
From PRINCIPLES OF EDUCATIONAL AND PSYCHOLOGICAL MEASUREMENT AND EVALUATION, Second edition, by Gilbert Sax. (c) 1980 by Wadsworth, Inc., Belmont California, 94002. Reprinted by permission of the publisher.
From HUMAN DEVELOPMENT AND LEARNING Second edition, by H.V. Perkins. (c) 1974 by Wadsworth, Inc., Belmont, California. Reprinted by permission of the publisher.
From PREPARATION OF ART by June King McFee (c) 1979 by Wadsworth, Belmont, California. Reprinted by permission of the author.

WARREN H. GREEN, INC., St. Louis, Missouri:
From THE HEALTH AND EDUCATION OF THE ECONOMICALLY DEPRIVED CHILD by Sol Adler, 1968, reprinted by permission of the publisher.